History of Australia

An Enthralling Journey through the Ancient Indigenous Cultures, European Settlement, Colonial Era, and Modern Times

© Copyright 2025 - All rights reserved.

The content contained within this book may not be reproduced, duplicated, or transmitted without direct written permission from the author or the publisher.

Under no circumstances will any blame or legal responsibility be held against the publisher, or author, for any damages, reparation, or monetary loss due to the information contained within this book, either directly or indirectly.

Legal Notice:

This book is copyright protected. It is only for personal use. You cannot amend, distribute, sell, use, quote, or paraphrase any part, or the content within this book, without the consent of the author or publisher.

Disclaimer Notice:

Please note the information contained within this document is for educational and entertainment purposes only. All effort has been executed to present accurate, up-to-date, reliable, and complete information. No warranties of any kind are declared or implied. Readers acknowledge that the author is not engaging in the rendering of legal, financial, medical, or professional advice. The content within this book has been derived from various sources. Please consult a licensed professional before attempting any techniques outlined in this book.

By reading this document, the reader agrees that under no circumstances is the author responsible for any losses, direct or indirect, that are incurred as a result of the use of the information contained within this document, including, but not limited to, errors, omissions, or inaccuracies.

Free limited time bonus

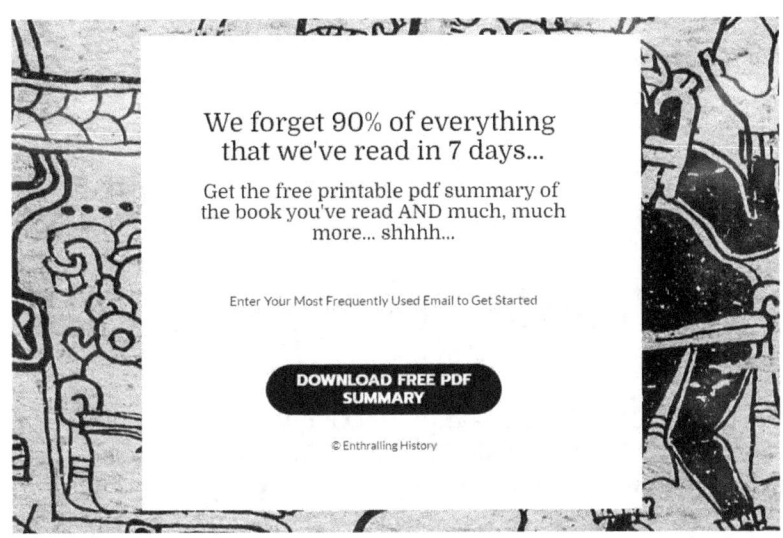

Stop for a moment. We have a free bonus set up for you. The problem is this: we forget 90% of everything that we read after 7 days. Crazy fact, right? Here's the solution: we've created a printable, 1-page pdf summary for this book that you're reading now. All you have to do to get your free pdf summary is to go to the following website: https://livetolearn.lpages.co/enthrallinghistory/

Or, Scan the QR code!

Once you do, it will be intuitive. Enjoy, and thank you!

Table of Contents

INTRODUCTION: AUSTRALIA—A COUNTRY THAT IS AS UNIQUE AS A PLATYPUS BEAK 1

CHAPTER 1: BEFORE AUSTRALIA WAS AUSTRALIA— INDIGENOUS ORIGINS 3

CHAPTER 2: DISCOVERY AND EXPLORATION: EUROPEAN ARRIVAL IN AUSTRALIA 11

CHAPTER 3: COLONIZATION AND CONVICTS: THE FOUNDING OF BRITISH SETTLEMENTS 20

CHAPTER 4: GOLD RUSH AND ECONOMIC BOOM: THE TRANSFORMATIVE 19TH CENTURY 34

CHAPTER 5: THE PUSH INLAND, FEDERATION, AND THE BIRTH OF AUSTRALIA 40

CHAPTER 6: WORLD WAR I AND AUSTRALIA'S INCREASING ROLE IN GLOBAL CONFLICTS 51

CHAPTER 7: THE INTERWAR PERIOD, ABORIGINAL RIGHTS, AND A STOLEN GENERATION 58

CHAPTER 8: AUSTRALIA DURING WORLD WAR II 63

CHAPTER 9: IMMIGRATION, REVITALIZATION, AND THE SHAPING OF MODERN AUSTRALIA 72

CHAPTER 10: THE ECONOMY AND ENVIRONMENTAL AND POLITICAL CHALLENGES 78

CONCLUSION: AUSTRALIA'S FUTURE FOREIGN POLICY 91

HERE'S ANOTHER BOOK BY ENTHRALLING HISTORY THAT YOU MIGHT LIKE 93

FREE LIMITED TIME BONUS 94

FURTHER READING AND REFERENCE 95
IMAGE SOURCES 96

Introduction: Australia — A Country That Is as Unique as a Platypus Beak

Perhaps it is the understatement of the century, but Australia has a rather unique history. Australia is also a rather unique place. This continent has some of the rarest flora and fauna on the planet. After all, Australia is home to a warm-blooded mammal that lays eggs. Everywhere else, that is strictly the business of reptiles and birds, but just try to tell that to the platypus!

The platypus is a marsupial. This critter is closely related to the porcupine, but it still has many unique features. Besides laying eggs, this animal carries a deadly venom. Throughout most of the world, animals like scorpions, spiders, and snakes carry venom. In Australia, a cute and cuddly platypus packs a deadly venomous punch. However, it would be more accurate to say kick in the case of the platypus. The hind legs of the animal produce the venom, and it is injected into its victim through special spurs on its back feet.

This animal is so strange, with its fur, duck-styled beak, beaver tail, reptile-like crawl, and otter-like feet, that many early biologists who were given dead specimens to examine insisted that the bodies had to have been fake. These esteemed scientists were absolutely certain that this Frankenstein beast just could not be real. They insisted that it must have been stitched together from the parts of several other creatures.

There is no other way to put it: this part of the world is one of a kind. This was one of the main draws for early European explorers. They wanted to learn more about this strange region. As time passed, Europeans settled in the area.

Captain Arthur Phillip, the man who is, in many ways, considered the founder of modern Australia, is certainly a polarizing figure. He planted a flag in Sydney Harbor in 1788, beginning widespread settlement of the region. Some hail him as a hero, while others decry him as a usurper who appropriated the lands of others.

Nevertheless, whether we love him or hate him, it is hard to deny his bold audacity. He sailed very far from his home and was determined to make do in (what was to them) an entirely alien land.

Phillip did this by choice. It is important to note that many others were brought to this strange land not by choice. For many years, convicted criminals were sent to Australia as punishment. Australia has had more than its fair share of sarcastic remarks about how it got its start as a penal colony, but such things are simply a part of Australian history.

The convicts might have initially been brought to this land against their will, but they learned to survive in this new terrain. Some of them even escaped the clutches of their taskmasters long enough to become so-called "bushrangers." These rough and tumble rebels, for all of their faults, are yet another strand in the fabric that makes up the Australian tapestry. From the real-life Ned Kelly to the fictional Crocodile Dundee, the notion of rugged individualists roughing it in the bush and making their own rules is the stuff of legend.

Yes, just like the platypus, Australia is the whole of many unique parts that seem to, impossibly enough, somehow complement each other despite being diametrically opposed.

Chapter 1: Before Australia Was Australia—Indigenous Origins

"This is what my father taught me and this is what I have to teach my sons, and my son has to teach his sons the same way as my father taught me. And that's the way it will go on from grandparents to sons, and follow that jukurrpa. No one knows when it will end."

-Paddy Japaljarri

About ten thousand years ago, the world was still firmly in an ice age. This was a geologic period in which much of the world's surface was either covered with ice or decidedly cooler than it is today. Even places that would be considered beachfront property now might have been rather chilly at times during this epoch.

We have to use the term "beaches" loosely because back in the Ice Age, the modern eye likely would not recognize much of the terrain of what we now refer to as Australia. The sea levels were much lower back then since much of the ocean water was frozen in glaciers. These low sea levels created land bridges between areas that would later be filled with all of that melted ice water.

The most famous example of this is the Bering land bridge, located between North America and Eurasia. It is full of water now, but when the water levels were lower, it is strongly believed that a land bridge

---

[1] Macintyre, Stuart. A Concise History of Australia. 1999. Pg. 10.

linked these two continents. Essentially, it would have been possible for a person to walk from Siberia to Alaska across this dry stretch of land. It has been theorized that this was how Native Americans first arrived in the Americas.

When it comes to Australia, there were a few land bridges that were of great importance. There was the Bassian Plain, which linked Australia to Tasmania, and there was the Sahul, which joined Australia to New Guinea. Both created corridors that would have allowed ancient Australians to travel overland to reach new regions to settle and explore.

In fact, it is believed that Australia was still connected to New Guinea by the Sahul land bridge as recently as eight thousand years ago.[i] That might seem like a long time ago, but in the long human history of Australia (which some say goes back at least sixty-five thousand years ago), it would be more like yesterday.[ii]

Scholars believe these low water levels and land bridges facilitated the first migrations to the landmass we now call Australia. The waters between Asia and Australia were much narrower, and island chains were much closer. Because of this, it is thought that the earliest people to arrive in Australia did so by navigating across these island chains in canoes.

Even the simplest of canoes could have sailed the short distances between islands until one reached Australia proper. This is backed up by many Indigenous legends that have been passed down countless generations. These tales speak of long treks across the water by canoe for various reasons and purposes.

The traditional way of life of the Indigenous people of Australia, better known as the Aboriginal people, has its own unique set of positive and negative aspects. There is no such thing as a perfect society; all cultures have what might be perceived as good virtues, as well as customs and cultural behaviors that might be perceived as bad. Of course, what constitutes good and bad is usually based on the perceptions of an outside, dominating culture.

Let's look at an example. Some of the Aboriginals of New Guinea, just north of the Australian continent, are said to have engaged in

---

[i] Macintyre, Stuart. A Concise History of Australia. 1999. Pg. 15.

[ii] Macintyre, Stuart. A Concise History of Australia. 1999. Pg. 9.

cannibalism. There is still some debate on this matter, but most scholars agree that cannibalism was indeed practiced at some point in New Guinea's history, something that none other than US President Joe Biden seemed to agree with.

Biden was visiting a war memorial site in Pennsylvania when his speech took a surprising turn. In a random offhand anecdote, he suggested that his uncle had been eaten by cannibals when he crashed his plane in New Guinea. Biden's uncle was a pilot during World War II, and he became marooned in a part of New Guinea. He was never heard from again.

Of course, the fact that such a thing was alluded to does not make them true, and it most certainly does not make them any less controversial. Shortly after Biden spoke those words, there was an immediate backlash. Even the prime minister of Papua New Guinea, James Marape, weighed in on the controversy. Prime Minister Marape stated that these misconceptions about Papua New Guinea were wrong and hurtful and should be avoided.

While Biden's remark became a point of controversy, it highlights a broader issue: long-standing Western misconceptions about Indigenous cultures in the Pacific region. For centuries, colonial narratives and sensationalized accounts have shaped how certain societies have been perceived. Early explorers and anthropologists often exaggerated or misunderstood Indigenous practices, sometimes portraying entire communities in a negative or exoticized light.

At any rate, it is safe to say that most of us today would frown upon any cultural practice that involves eating people. As far as we know, no Indigenous tribe practices cannibalism today. Such things are not seen as an acceptable cultural trait by the vast majority of the world now, any more than it was considered acceptable hundreds of years ago.

It is believed that only a small portion of the Aboriginal people actually engaged in cannibalism. It has become somewhat of a norm to paint Indigenous people with the same brush. However, we have to understand that the Aboriginals were made up of many diverse tribes that all had their own unique cultures. One tribe might have practiced cannibalism, and another tribe might have been horrified by it.

All cultural perceptions aside, the Aboriginal people of Australia can certainly be proud of the fact that their ancestors were even able to find their way to Australia in the first place. It is believed that the first

Aboriginal people arrived in Australia around sixty thousand years ago. The Aboriginal people are one of the oldest continuous cultures on Earth.

The first Aboriginal people arrived during the last Ice Age. Australia was a lot different back then. When these newcomers arrived in this strange new land, they had to find a means to eke out a sustainable existence. The first people of Australia had to be smart and able to think on their feet. After all, they were encountering what was basically a new world of unknown flora and fauna.

Although the later European explorers often get a lot of credit for their daring missions over the high seas to get to Australia, this should not diminish the bravery of the earliest Australian explorers. They also faced a new and alien world. Upon reaching Australia, they encountered incredible species of animals, some of which no longer exist. They might have encountered a giant variation of the kangaroo that is said to have been nearly three meters (almost ten feet) tall. They also likely encountered the now-extinct *Diprotodon*, which was a relative of the wombat and the size of a modern-day rhinoceros.[i]

The Aboriginals likely sampled the local plants and animals with caution at first, but over time, they became accustomed to the resources this island continent had to offer. For example, the *Diprotodon* became a favorite target of hunters. In fact, the large marsupial, which went extinct some twenty-five thousand years ago, is believed to have been overhunted by the Aboriginals, similar to how the Native Americans are thought to have brought about the end of the giant sloth in North America. The giant sloth of North America and the *Diprotodon* of Australia did not have much defense against human hunters. So, when bands of humans showed up and began mercilessly cornering the beasts and making them a regular food source, they were most likely driven to extinction as a result.

The fact that the emergence of humans in a new, untouched environment led to the extinction of animals is not surprising. As author and historian Geoffrey Blainey put it, the arrival of humans "into new regions is usually accompanied by the extinction of species."[ii]

---

[i] Blainey, Geoffrey. *A Shorter History of Australia*. 1994. Pg. 6.

[ii] Blainey, Geoffrey. *A Shorter History of Australia*. 1994. Pg. 6.

The Aboriginals were not known to store food, so their population level is not believed to have been very high. Storing food is a necessary step for sustaining a larger population. Otherwise, groups of humans are limited by the resources that can be hunted or gathered at the time.

Another facet of Aboriginal life that is often missed by many historians is the impact of tribal warfare. Some might feel inclined to depict the ancient Aboriginal people as peaceful, but this is not an accurate depiction. It defies both the common history of humanity and its general push toward violence, as well as the history of the Aboriginals in particular.

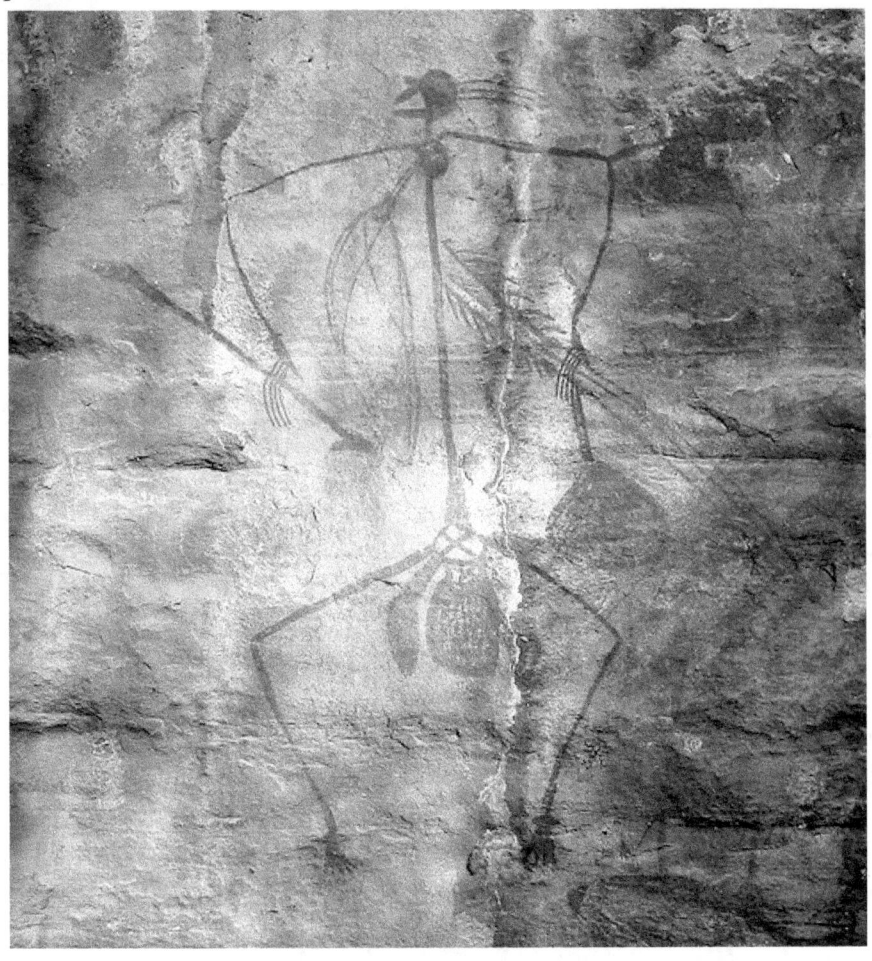

Aboriginal rock art.[1]

It has long been known that vengeance killing among the Aboriginals was common. Sometimes, superstitious beliefs led to massacres. If a person perished from some terrible disease or illness, one could ascribe the death to evil spirits. They could even say that those evil spirits had been summoned by a tribal enemy. Of course, such beliefs defy the logic of most of us today, but this was a common practice among the Aboriginals in the past. If one group seriously believed that another group had utilized spirits to kill one of their tribe, it could trigger an all-out war between the two tribal groups.

A spate of intertribal warfare was documented by outside sources as late as 1875. During that year, a great massacre took place in central Australia among the Aboriginals, which is said to have left nearly one hundred dead and many more injured.[i] No one seems to know what started this conflict, but it could have been sparked by a perceived slight. These episodes of violence would have also served to curb the population growth among the Aboriginals of Australia.

As it pertains to the overall population of the ancient Aboriginals, some scholars have floated numbers like one million, but such a thing seems doubtful. Most scholars peg the peak population of Aboriginals to be closer to 500,000 at most. It is estimated that this is likely the maximum number of people that could be sustained on a hunter-gatherer lifestyle in Australia.

The term "hunter-gatherer" can be viewed as both a term of historical significance for humanity as a whole, as well as a vocation of the Aboriginals in particular. It is believed that all of humanity went through a hunter-gatherer stage at some point. It was only when civilizations began to settle down and plant crops that farming replaced hunting and gathering as the main source of food. The rise of farming allowed for more controlled resources and more complex versions of societies.

Rather than living out in the bush chasing any rabbit they saw, people were able to establish long-term settlements where all of their needs were readily provided for them. This also established a firm hierarchy, in which some were categorized as being of a higher rank than others. These distinctions left a mark.

When Europeans encountered the Aboriginals centuries later, they tended to look down on them as being part of the lowest rung of society. The roots of their subsequent prejudice can be found here.

---

[i] Blainey, Geoffrey. *A Shorter History of Australia*. 1994. Pg. 10.

The European explorers believed those they encountered were destined to adopt their ways and leave behind what they considered the primitive backwaters of a hunter-gatherer civilization. But what many of these first European explorers failed to realize was that the hunter-gatherer lifestyle of the Aboriginals had become perfectly balanced and adapted to the environment in which they lived.

Later anthropologists would come to see this prejudiced misconception as being rather flawed in light of the fact that the Aboriginals lived just fine within the confines of their hunter-gatherer society for tens of thousands of years.[i]

It has been estimated that the average lifespan of an Aboriginal was likely fifty years. This was due to a wide variety of reasons, such as illness, environmental factors, and violence.

In regard to environmental factors, the mighty El Niño effect likely created a lot of the environmental hardships that Indigenous Australians faced. El Niño induced droughts, which left the eastern two-thirds of the continent periodically parched. These long droughts likely made the Indigenous people conclude long ago that sedentary farming was not a practical means of sustenance in their harsh environment.[ii]

Despite these environmental challenges, the Aboriginals proved to be tenacious and ingenious as it pertained to how they handled these difficulties. The Aboriginal people were always on the move. A mother with young children would have found mobility a bit difficult. Yet, someone, somewhere along the way, must have looked at the kangaroo hopping around with a baby in its pouch and gotten an idea. The Aboriginals began to take kangaroo skins to fashion their own makeshift kangaroo pouches, which women would put over their backs so that they could walk while carrying their babies with ease.[iii]

It is believed that these early residents utilized the native gum trees for kindling. These early Australians sat around campfires, which they used to keep warm and for lighting. As the indigenous peoples of Australia sat around these campfires, they were able to lean back and wonder. Like any human on the planet who is given ample time to think about

---

[i] Macintyre, Stuart. A Concise History of Australia. 1999. Pg. 13.

[ii] Macintyre, Stuart. A Concise History of Australia. 1999. Pg. 15.

[iii] Blainey, Geoffrey. *A Shorter History of Australia.* 1994. Pg. 7.

themselves and their condition, philosophical notions began to come to mind.

The Aboriginal people began to ask deep and meaningful questions. "Who are we? How did we get here?" they mused to themselves. In order to answer these puzzling questions, they began to develop their own personal belief systems.

Today, anthropologists would likely refer to these as creation myths. However, it is important to realize that for the people who developed these beliefs, they were not myths at all.

While these beliefs might sound strange to outsiders, they made sense to Native Australians. In fact, many Native people of Australia still believe in the Aboriginal concept of the Dreaming. Now, to be clear, we are not speaking about those strange snippets of the subconscious mind we experience when we lay down to sleep in our beds. Instead, the Dreaming refers to an ancient and ongoing spiritual belief that the world was created through the dreams and actions of supernatural beings. Their dreamy thoughts carved out rivers and pushed up mountains. Their dreams conceived of plants and animals of all kinds, including human beings. Aboriginal belief contends that since we are all made of this same basic dream essence, there is a certain mutability as it pertains to everything else that exists. There is a belief that one form of life and existence can merge and blend with another. Even so, honoring one's ancestors and what came before is considered crucially important.[i]

In Stuart Macintyre's book, *A Concise History of Australia*, an Aboriginal elder by the name of Paddy Japaljarri Stewart describes a kind of "dream maintenance" that Aboriginal believers feel compelled (perhaps even responsible) in maintaining, lest the dream should end, and their culture and tradition fade away.

---

[i] Macintyre, Stuart. A Concise History of Australia. 1999. Pg. 9.

Chapter 2: Discovery and Exploration: European Arrival in Australia

"From what I have said of the Natives of New Holland, they may appear to some to be the most wretched people upon the Earth, but in reality, they are far more happier than we Europeans; being wholly unacquainted not only with the superfluous but the necessary Conveniences so much sought after in Europe, they are happy in not knowing the use of them. They live in a Tranquility which is not disturb'd by the inequality of condition; the Earth and sea of their own accord furnishes them with all things necessary for life."

-Captain James Cook[1]

We have to be very careful when we speak of the "discovery" of Australia. We have to recognize that the island had already been discovered by other groups of people before the Europeans arrived. We must realize that when we speak of discovery in these terms, we are more specifically speaking of the Europeans' discovery.

There is actually some debate over which European power first discovered Australia. It has long been suggested that the Dutch held this honor, although some have suggested that it was the Portuguese. The

---

[1] Macintyre, Stuart. A Concise History of Australia. 1999. Pg. 28.

debate over whether it was the Dutch or the Portuguese who first stumbled onto Australia is understandable considering how competitive these two European powers were at the time.

The Portuguese were the first to round the tip of South Africa; they achieved this milestone in 1488. This opened a new route to India, as they could circumnavigate around the tip of South Africa and then head northeast through the Indian Ocean. This kickstarted a push for further European exploration of India and other parts of the world that had previously been hard to reach. The Dutch were close on the heels of the Portuguese and explored many of the same regions that the Portuguese did.

Some say that the Portuguese from their southeastern Asian island outpost of Timor, where they established a base in 1516, occasionally had ships driven off-course. They perhaps caught sight of the northwestern coast of Australia as a result.[i] If so, they did not attempt to do much to pursue that mysterious coastline.

In 1605, Portuguese explorer Pedro Fernández de Quirós, sailing under the Spanish Crown, led an expedition in search of the great southern land (Terra Australis), a vast, semi-mythical continent that many Europeans believed lay hidden in the Southern Hemisphere. Convinced that they were on the brink of discovering this uncharted territory, the Spaniards envisioned it as a new land ready for exploration, bestowing upon it the grand title Australia del Espíritu Santo ("Southern Land of the Holy Spirit").

When Quirós reached the New Hebrides (modern-day Vanuatu), he named the largest island La Austrialia del Espíritu Santo, intentionally modifying the spelling to honor King Philip III of Spain, who belonged to the House of Austria. Believing he had finally set foot on the legendary southern continent, Quirós announced his discovery with great enthusiasm. However, in reality, he had only reached an island, falling short of the vast landmass he had hoped to find.

As far as we know, it was the Dutch who etched the first reliable record of Australia into history. In 1606, a ship under the command of the Dutch East India Company (VOC), called the *Duyfken*, a name that translates roughly as "Little Dove," became the first known European vessel to make landfall on the Australian mainland.

---

[i] Blainey, Geoffrey. *A Shorter History of Australia*. 1994. Pg. 23.

The *Duyfken* was captained by Willem Janszoon, who, along with his crew, charted approximately 320 kilometers (200 miles) of coastline along the Cape York Peninsula (modern-day Queensland). At the time, they mistakenly believed they were exploring part of New Guinea, not a new continent. Janszoon's voyage also marked the first recorded European encounter with Indigenous Australians, including a hostile skirmish that resulted in casualties among his crew.

While Janszoon's maps were limited, his landing in 1606 remains a milestone in European exploration, predating James Cook's famous 1770 voyage by more than 160 years.

Later that year, a former deputy of Pedro Fernandes de Queirós, Luís Vaz de Torres, made his way toward Australia along the Torres Strait (which was subsequently named after him) from New Guinea. Although Torres laid sight on the Australian mainland, he most likely did not realize just how expansive the land was.

Still, it was the Dutch who led the charge as it pertained to mapping out Australia. A Dutch explorer named Dirk Hartog initially ended up doing so by accident. In 1616, he found himself off course after rounding the Cape of Good Hope en route to Batavia. Back in those days, Batavia was the capital of the Dutch East Indies. It would later become the Indonesian capital, Jakarta.

At any rate, this crew that launched off from Batavia found itself landing near the western portion of Australia's coastline known as Shark Bay. It must be stressed that they landed near Australia and not on it. They actually landed on a nearby island. However, Australia was within sight, and it would not be long until many more landings would be made.

In 1622 (some say 1623), a ship called the *Leeuwin*—Dutch for "Lioness"—set anchor on the southwestern coast of Australia. Though few records of this voyage remain, it is believed that the crew charted parts of the coastline in what is now Western Australia. The headland they encountered would later be named Cape Leeuwin in honor of this fateful journey. Unlike other Dutch expeditions that focused on the northern and western coasts, this voyage marked one of the earliest European encounters with Australia's southwestern region.

A few years later, in 1627, another Dutch navigator, François Thijssen, took exploration a step further. Sailing aboard the *Gulden Zeepaert* ("Golden Seahorse"), Thijssen became the first European to chart much of Australia's southern coast. He and his crew mapped over

1,800 kilometers (1,100 miles) of coastline, revealing a landmass stretching far beyond what was previously thought.

In the following year, 1628, a whole Dutch squadron was sent by the governor-general of the Dutch East Indies himself, Pieter de Carpentier. This expedition was tasked with taking a look at the continent's northern coastline. Many great discoveries were made during this particular expedition, including the discovery and subsequent naming of the Gulf of Carpentaria.

As you may have already guessed, this gulf was named after Pieter de Carpentier. Yes, everyone was quite eager to literally make a name for themselves as they discovered or commissioned new expeditions to new and extraordinary lands that had never been seen by European eyes before. It also must be noted that though these voyages expanded the Dutch understanding of the region, the Dutch never attempted to settle the land. Instead, their discoveries laid the groundwork for later explorers.

European explorers also paid attention to the surrounding region. One of the most significant figures in this effort was Abel Tasman. In 1642, sailing under the flag of the Dutch East India Company (VOC), Tasman set out on an expedition to further explore the unknown lands beyond the Indies.

Abel Tasman.[2]

Later that year, Tasman and his crew became the first Europeans to lay eyes on the landmass we now call Tasmania—an island off the southern coast of Australia. He named it Van Diemen's Land after Antonio van Diemen, the governor-general of the Dutch East Indies. Pushing farther east, Tasman went on to become the first known European to reach New Zealand, though his attempt to land there ended in conflict with the Māori, resulting in the deaths of several of his men.

Tasman never actually sighted the Australian mainland, but his voyage was still groundbreaking. He helped solidify the Dutch understanding of the southern lands, and his maps later played a role in shaping European knowledge of the region. Tasman became the first to call Australia by the name New Holland. Decades later, Dutch cartographers would apply the name New Holland to Australia, cementing the legacy of the Dutch in the early mapping of the continent.

In fact, these efforts led to the near-complete mapping of most of Australia and the surrounding region by 1648. This map was put together by a Dutch mapmaker named Joan Blaeu and was dubbed the "Nova et Accuratissima Totius Terrarum Orbis Tabula."

The British were not about to let the Dutch have all the glory, and in 1688, a British explorer—and part-time pirate—William Dampier, made his way to Australia's northwest coast. Dampier was serving aboard the *Cygnet*, a ship full of privateers-turned-pirates who had spent the past few years plundering Spanish territories and raiding vessels across the Pacific. Unlike the Dutch explorers who had mapped Australia with official backing, Dampier and his crew arrived by accident, looking for a quiet place to repair their ship.

After sailing through Indonesia, they made landfall near King Sound (modern-day Western Australia). Dampier became one of the first Englishmen to step foot on Australian soil. While his visit was not part of an official British effort to claim Australia, it marked the beginning of British interest in the continent. A decade later, Dampier returned—this time, not as a pirate, but as a government-backed explorer.

William Dampier took it upon himself to document the land and its inhabitants in great detail. In 1703, he published his book, *A Voyage to New Holland*, in which he recounted his experiences exploring the northwestern coast of Australia. Dampier's descriptions of the land were vivid. He noted the barren, dry landscapes, the strange flora, and the unfamiliar wildlife, including large hopping creatures that would later be recognized as kangaroos (this word originates from the Guugu Yimithirr word *gangurru*).

More notably, Dampier was also among the first Europeans to write about the Indigenous Australians. He described them as "the miserablest people in the world," commenting on their lack of clothing, houses, and European-style agriculture. From his European perspective, he saw their nomadic lifestyle as a sign of poverty rather than an adaptation to their environment. He remarked on their dark skin, curly hair, and thin physiques, noting that they seemed to survive primarily by fishing and foraging. Though Dampier acknowledged their skill in hunting and their use of spears, his harsh and dismissive descriptions reflected the biases of his time.

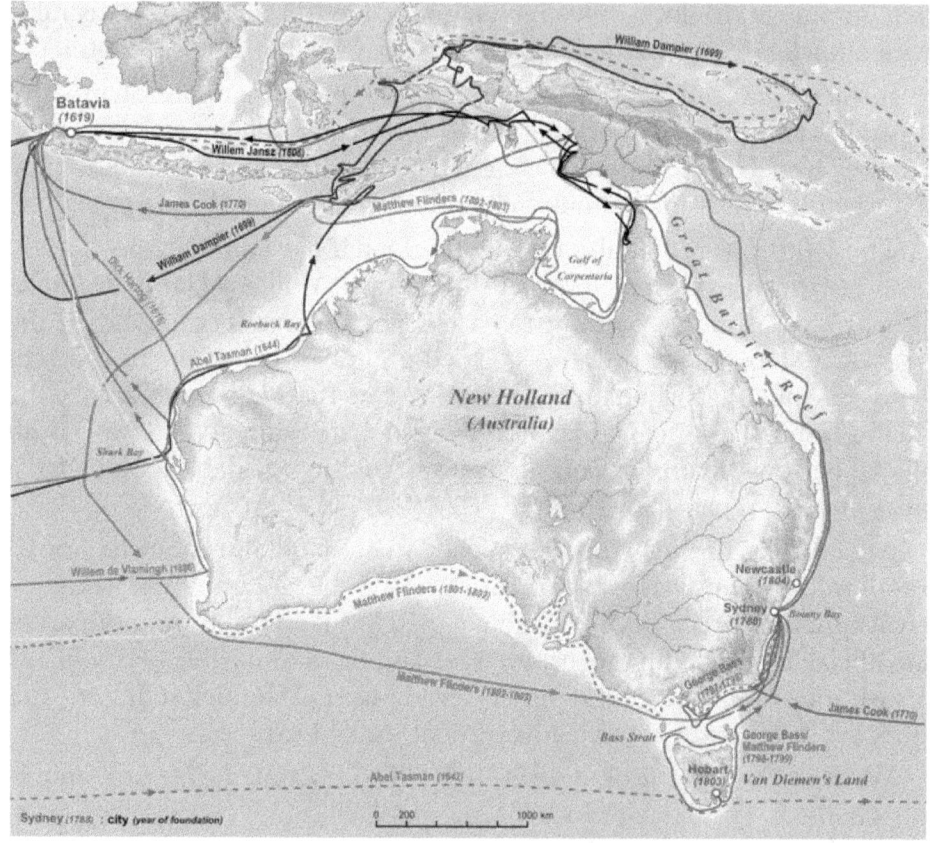

Voyages of European explorers before 1813.[3]

The later voyages of Englishman James Cook built upon much of what Dampier and others had discovered. James Cook was in the British navy and was the captain of the HMS *Endeavor*. In 1769, he and his crew embarked upon a mission to Tahiti, supposedly to take note of the transit of Venus as the planet traversed across the sky.

This was not the first time that Cook had been involved in observing astronomical events. In 1766, he had been part of a team that documented a solar eclipse, the transit of which had been viewed over Newfoundland in North America.

The task of documenting the transit of Venus from Tahiti was officially commissioned by Britain's esteemed scientific body, the Royal Society. Oxford scholar and professional botanist Joseph Banks tagged along with the crew. The observation of the transit of Venus was a milestone of great importance for science since the distance between the Earth and the sun could be made using these observations for the first time in history.[i]

There was, however, an ulterior motive at work. Along with charting the course of Venus, Cook had secret orders to see if he could reach Australia and perhaps make a claim on the land for the British.

The British had been largely shut out of Australia by this point. Since other European powers had already sunk their teeth into the continent, Cook had to be very discreet about how he undertook his exploration/conquest of Australia.

On April 19th, 1770, Captain James Cook and his men spied land off the southeastern coast of Australia at a place he later named Point Hicks. They continued sailing northward and, on April 28th, 1770, entered a large bay where the landscape was described by Cook as "as fine a meadow as ever was seen." The bay was initially called Stingray Bay, but after botanists Joseph Banks and Daniel Solander collected an astonishing variety of plants, it was renamed Botany Bay.

Cook then embarked on a harrowing journey up the northeastern coast, charting the land and making periodic landfalls. At times, his men carved marks into trees to leave signs of their journey. However, the expedition nearly ended in disaster on June 11th, 1770. Cook's ship, the *Endeavour*, struck a coral reef—part of what is now known as the Great Barrier Reef. The ship took on water, but after a desperate struggle, Cook and his crew managed to beach and repair it at Endeavour River, where they remained for seven weeks.

---

[i] Blainey, Geoffrey. *A Shorter History of Australia*. 1994. Pg. 25.

Despite the challenges, Cook pressed onward. On August 22nd, 1770, he landed on Possession Island in the Torres Strait, where he formally claimed the entire eastern coast of Australia for Britain, naming it New South Wales. His voyage would later set the stage for British colonization, forever changing the course of Australia's history.

Interestingly, Cook's earliest observations of the region were glowingly positive, with little inclination of the hardships that later explorers would face. Unbeknownst to Cook, he had landed in the middle of what was Australia's rainy season. This was a time when the soil would appear much more fertile than during the dry season, and water, in the form of flowing streams, would be present.

James Cook marveled at what he thought was rich and robust grasslands. He suggested that the grasslands were so great that cattle could graze there all year round. Considering his glowing description, later explorers who arrived in the land during the dry season were shocked to find a parched hellscape with little resemblance to anything like what James Cook had described.[i]

Captain James Cook.[*]

---

[i] Blainey, Geoffrey. *A Shorter History of Australia*. 1994. Pg. 25.

Britain had its hands full at the time. Its colonies in North America were on the verge of a full-out rebellion. These thirteen colonies would soon declare war against Britain.

Against all odds, the upstart colonists won the war, forming the United States of America and forcing the British to admit defeat in 1783. After Britain lost most of its territory along the Atlantic coast of North America, it began to take a serious look at Australia. Britain's Home Office issued a document in 1786 that established Botany Bay as a site for potential settlement. This document also outlined the grand scheme of transforming Australia's Botany Bay into a penal colony, a decision that would have ramifications for many generations to come.[i]

Why this particular spot was chosen is still debated. It could be that it was simply the most well-trod spot on the coast by the British at this point in time. It has also been argued that the British felt the region put them in a strategically advantageous position as it pertained to the Dutch East Indies, which was located nearby. It is also argued that the location had plenty of much-needed resources, such as flax, timber, and even whales. Others, however, contend that the British merely wanted to send their undesirables as far away as possible.

This is, of course, a rather simplistic and cynical view, but its premise is a logical one, albeit based on hindsight since we know that Britain would indeed send many prisoners to Australia.

---

[i] Macintyre, Stuart. A Concise History of Australia. 1999. Pg. 28.

Chapter 3: Colonization and Convicts: The Founding of British Settlements

"The truth is, of course, that my own people, the Riratjungi, are descended from the great Djankawa who came from the island of Baralku, far across the sea. Our spirits return to Baralku when we die. Djankawa came in his canoe with his two sisters, following the morning star which guided them to the shores of Yelangbara on the eastern coast of Arnhem Land. They walked far across the country following the rain clouds. When they wanted water they plunged their digging stick into the ground and fresh water followed. From them we learnt the names of all the creatures on the land and they taught us all our Law."

-Wandjuk Marika[i]

Although some historians insist that the portrayal of Australia's founding as a penal colony is somewhat overblown, there is still plenty of truth to be found in such assertions. Numerous convicts did indeed arrive to live in the early settlement located near Australia's Port Jackson.

The port had been established in Sydney Harbor and was named after Sir George Jackson, who had served as the lord commissioner of the British Admiralty. This port eventually became the staging grounds

---

[i] Macintyre, Stuart. A Concise History of Australia. 1999. Pg. 9.

of a grand experiment in forced labor and settlement.

Those who had been convicted of crimes back home in Britain, which included prostitution, theft, and even murder, were sentenced to exile in Australia. Once they arrived, they would be forced to help build what would later become a bustling colony.

Their legacy has lasting repercussions that can be felt to this very day. A sizeable number of modern-day Australians descended from convicts, and many of these descendants are actually quite famous. For instance, former Prime Minister Kevin Rudd is descended from a colonial convict.

In 1788, Britain's First Fleet arrived on Australian shores in force. Captain Arthur Phillip was established as the governor-general of the fledgling colony. Arthur Phillip and company had left Britain in May 1787 with eleven ships. On board these vessels were sailors, convicts, marines, and officers. All of them were forced to live in cramped quarters for the duration of the trip.

A portrait of Arthur Phillip.[5]

The journey from Britain to Australia was, of course, quite an adventure, and along the way, the First Fleet made several important stops. Their first stop was at the Canary Islands (Tenerife), where they rested for a week before continuing southwestward to Rio de Janeiro, Brazil. There, the fleet docked for about a month, allowing the crew to rest, repair ships, and resupply before setting sail once more.

After departing Brazil, Governor Arthur Phillip and his crew took a southeasterly course to the tip of South Africa, where they docked at Cape Town for another month. These were all foreign-controlled ports, and as such, the British had to tread carefully. Although they had nothing to fear from the Portuguese authorities in Brazil or the Dutch in South Africa, they were still guests in these lands and had to respect local rules. Britain's biggest rival at the time was France, but even in neutral ports, Phillip made sure his men remained disciplined to avoid any trouble that might delay their historic journey.

After spending a month in Cape Town, Arthur Phillip and his fleet sailed off. The First Fleet finally reached its destination at Botany Bay some eight months after it first departed from British territory. The fleet carried around 443 naval personnel, 759 convicts, and 160 or so marines, the latter of whom were tasked with keeping the convicts in line.

As you may suspect, the prisoners did not have much say in the matter, but many of them were led to believe they were being taken to a veritable paradise, a land of great bounty. Furthermore, they had been promised that in exchange for working and tilling the fields, they would eventually secure their own freedom.

Of course, this idyllic picture was far from what these souls actually experienced upon their arrival in January 1788. Australia was not the paradise that had been described, and their existence would be a hard one. Initially, every day was a struggle just to keep going.

The First Fleet set anchor during the region's harshest season, right in the midst of a scorching summer. The absence of rainfall had turned the ground into a dry, scorching hellscape. Clean water was very difficult to come by, so all the resources had to be carefully rationed among the settlers.

Nevertheless, on January 26th, 1788, British flags were raised over the port that became part of a new settlement called Sydney. It was named in honor of British Secretary of State Lord Sydney. This day—simply known as Australia Day— has since been heralded as the moment that modern Australia was founded. However, for those whose ancestors already lived in the region before the British arrived to settle the land, this day would come to be known as Invasion Day. In their eyes, this was the day that a foreign force took hold of their ancestral lands and changed the lives of those who dwelled there forever.

The first real change the Aboriginals faced came in the form of diseases spread by the newcomers. These settlers—whether they realized it or not—carried pathogens that the isolated Aboriginal people had never encountered. Their immune systems had no defense against these viruses. Of all the pestilences that were brought to Australia, the dreaded disease known as smallpox was the worst. Smallpox is believed to have decimated at least half of the local population in a very short time after its introduction. Some estimates state around 80 percent of the Aboriginal population was killed by European diseases. According to historian and scholar Barbara West, the disease took only a matter of months to lay waste to these Indigenous Australian communities.

As much as the Aboriginals suffered, it would be both wrong and perhaps a disservice to paint them as merely defenseless spectators to the arrival of the British. On the contrary, they were active participants, and there were times they decided to strike back against those who had dared to occupy their land. At one point, Governor-General Arthur Phillip was ambushed by some locals and had a spear hurled into his shoulder. It has been said that Phillip ran for cover with the spear still protruding from his arm. Fortunately for him, it was just a flesh wound, and the injury did not become infected.

A depiction of the Aboriginals from 1784.[6]

Despite being injured like this, Phillip—unlike what many others might have done—refused to take any retaliatory action. He seemed to realize that what had happened to him was likely a (rather painful) misunderstanding and did not want to escalate the situation any further. This is a sign of smart leadership, as one should be able to pick and choose their battles.

Phillip eventually achieved some rather promising relations with the locals. Interestingly enough, the fact that he was missing one of his teeth actually aided him in this regard. It was an Aboriginal tradition for older, more esteemed members of the tribe to yank one of their front teeth out. It was seen as a special rite of passage.

So, when it was noticed that Phillip was missing a tooth, the Aboriginals saw it as a sign that he was an elder. He was seen as someone who was somewhat familiar with their culture and traditions. It was an ironic coincidence, but it managed to help smooth over relations that otherwise might have been much more difficult.

The Aboriginals were more than willing to show their teeth to the British. The British, of course, had the Aboriginals outgunned, so the Aboriginals did not have the capacity to launch a major offensive against them. As such, their attempts to push back against the colonizers took the shape of intermittent ambushes, such as the one Governor-General Arthur Phillip experienced.

Besides the threat of these occasional acts of violence, by far the most challenging aspect of these early settlers' lives was making sure they did not starve to death. The British brought a lot of supplies with them, but these supplies would only last for so long. Additionally, the supply ships did not always make it to Australia. For example, the British supply ship HMS *Guardian* set out from South Africa's Cape of Good Hope, only to find itself off-course in the southern seas. It slammed into an iceberg.

The loss of the HMS *Guardian* meant that extra food and supplies would not be arriving anytime soon. This meant that the Second Fleet would have to make do with what they already had, and the people would also have to do what they could to start growing their own crops once they reached land.[i]

---

[i] West, Barbara A. *A Brief History of Australia*. 2010. Pg. 42.

In June of 1790, the British Second Fleet made its way to Port Jackson with some rudimentary supplies and 733 more prisoners.

Due to the lack of enough supplies to go around for all of these newcomers, it became imperative to find ways to cultivate the lands of Australia. In an effort to further this cause, important farming tools were imported, such as plows, hoes, shovels, axes, and the like. This hardened prisoner workforce was handed these tools and expected to do the back-breaking labor of cutting away foliage, digging up the soil, and planting crops.

One of the first major setbacks they faced was a bad batch of seeds. The convicts had planted seeds for crops, but when they did not seem to take root, the British cast a wary eye toward the Dutch traders whom they had purchased them from. These seeds had been bought from the Dutch at the Cape of Good Hope and then brought to Australia. The British wondered if their sometimes rival, the Dutch, had purposefully sabotaged the seeds. Such things are possible, but it is also possible that Australia's harsh and often challenging environment was the culprit.

The rationing of food became even more severe as the colony struggled to survive. To prevent food supplies from being pilfered, Governor Arthur Phillip implemented harsh laws, making theft of rations a capital offense. Though this might seem extreme, one must consider the dire circumstances—the colony's food supply was dangerously low, and without strict rationing, everyone would have starved. Several convicts were executed for stealing food, as even a small theft could mean weeks of hunger for others.

In November 1788, the British established Parramatta, located farther inland from Sydney, in an attempt to find better farmland. Like Sydney, Parramatta began as a penal settlement, but it was intended to serve as an agricultural hub to support the struggling colony. However, both settlements faced severe shortages, and tensions ran high. Many of the convicts had been transported for theft, and in a colony where food was more valuable than gold, some were willing to risk their lives to steal it.

Along with the threat that they faced from within, the convict settlers also had to deal with an outside threat. Most of the interactions with the Aboriginals were initially few and far between. But as the settlers began to set down permanent roots, the clashes became more frequent. The biggest eruption of tensions occurred in 1790 in an incident known as Pemulwuy's War.

The war is named after an Aboriginal man who was seen as the spiritual leader of the conflict. Chief Pemulwuy is thought to have been around forty years of age when the conflict erupted. Pemulwuy and his band of warriors waged what was essentially a guerilla war against the settlers. Those who dared to set foot in the colony had to do so while constantly looking over their shoulder. This was especially the case if they ventured too far from the main settlements. Pemulwuy and his warriors were very familiar with the terrain, so they had an advantage in the fight.

This outbreak of fighting only came to an end in 1802 after Pemulwuy was shot to death. Demonstrating how much of a nemesis he was to the settlers, those who killed him made sure to cut off his head so they could send it back to their colonial taskmasters as proof that the chief was indeed dead.

A Scene of South Australia depicting German immigrants interacting with Aboriginals.[7]

In the midst of all of this fighting, colonial life continued. Farms and homesteads were maintained. During this period, livestock became a great boon to the settlers of Australia.

By 1795, nearly seven hundred sheep were dispersed among several farms near Sydney and Parramatta, marking the beginning of Australia's sheep farming industry. Just a few years later, by 1799, the colony's sheep population had grown to an estimated 4,588. Most of these early sheep were imported from South Africa's Cape Colony, but they were mainly used for meat rather than wool production.

Transporting livestock across such vast distances was incredibly costly and difficult, as settlers had to battle what historian Geoffrey Blainey later called the "tyranny of distance." With Australia being a remote outpost of the British Empire, supplies from Europe or even South Africa took months to arrive. Settlers had to make the most of the land available, focusing their farms along the fertile river valleys and coastal plains near Sydney, Parramatta, and the Hawkesbury River.[i]

In 1797, the colony took a major step toward becoming a wool-producing powerhouse when Merino sheep, originally from Spain, were introduced via South Africa. These sheep, prized for their fine wool, would lay the foundation for Australia's future as a world leader in wool production.

The cultivation of land was not the only thing that was encouraged. People were strongly encouraged to raise families. Marriage was made a top priority among both convicts and free settlers, as the colony needed a stable population to survive.

For most convicts, however, being sent to Australia meant permanent separation from their families. While many had wives and children back in Britain, they were not automatically entitled to have them sent over. Convicts were expected to serve their time alone, and many never saw their loved ones again.

That said, over time, some well-behaved convicts who had earned their freedom or received a "ticket of leave" were allowed to petition the government to bring their wives and children to Australia. This practice became more common under Governor Lachlan Macquarie in the 1810s as the colony shifted toward a free-settler economy. By the 1830s and 1840s, government-assisted migration schemes also helped bring over wives and children of former convicts.

---

[i] West, Barbara A. *A Brief History of Australia*. 2010. Pg. 10.

Though reunification was possible for a fortunate few, for many transported convicts, the price of their crimes was not just exile but the loss of their families as well.

The British realized marriage was important for the settlement of the colony for a wide variety of reasons. For one thing, a family structure provided stability and incentive for those who labored in the harsh Australian terrain to continue to work hard. They would not only work for their harsh British taskmasters but also for their own families, who depended upon their support.

Religion was also viewed as a fundamental pillar of the society that was being built, although unlike in previous colonial exercises, the exact type of religion that was to be embraced was left fairly vague. Britain had faced many years of tumult between Protestants and Catholics and even infighting between different Protestant denominations. In Australia, the settlers practiced many different Christian faiths. Initially, most settlers were Protestant, but in 1791, a massive influx of Irish Catholic convicts arrived. The Irish are said to have made up the largest group of established immigrants to Australia, with the exception of the English themselves, until the outbreak of World War I in 1914.

Many of these Irish prisoners had been convicted of the same sort of crimes as the other forced laborers in Australia, but there were some who had been convicted of a different sort of crime. They had been convicted of political crimes. Ireland had long been struggling against British rule, and many would-be revolutionaries were imprisoned. Some of these political prisoners inevitably found themselves in Australia.

However, it must be made clear that not all settlers were convicts during this period. As early as 1793, free settlers started to arrive in Australia. They arrived in fairly small numbers at first, but they would increase over time. These free settlers and the military officers stationed in Australia would forge a new class. These settlers and officers seemed naturally dispositioned to lord it over the rest.

This class of perceived elites was known as the Exclusives. The convicts were, by the nature of their conviction, made subservient to this free Australian class. Even after they had served the duration of their sentence, they and their offspring still had the sting of their previous poor reputation.

The arrival of a new governor-general—Lachlan Macquarie— in 1810 changed all of this. Macquarie was a no-nonsense lieutenant colonel who sought to establish law and order in light of previous unrest among military officers, the most notable of which was the Rum Rebellion, which shook up the whole colony in 1808.

On January 26th, 1808, on what was the twentieth anniversary of the settlement of Australia, Major George Johnston, who was in charge of the New South Wales Corps, headed a group of some four hundred troops in an attempt to overthrow the colonial government. These rebels managed to storm into the compound where Governor William Bligh was holed up and placed him under their custody.

William Bligh.'

This all-out mutiny had erupted after Governor Bligh banned the bartering of rum for food or wages. Prior to Bligh's ultimatum, rum had been used among the settlers as a form of currency. It was believed that this free-flowing alcohol was corrupting free and convict settlers alike. In a move to ensure discipline, Bligh forbade the practice.

By this point, most of the settlers already had a bad opinion of Bligh. He was viewed as being way too heavy-handed, and this last draconian command was seen as the last straw. So, Bligh was not just overruled; he was overthrown. The rebellion would be short-lived, though. Once the British Crown heard about it, the troops were forced to disband, and Major Johnston was arrested. Bligh found himself out of a job. He was ultimately replaced by Lachlan Macquarie as governor.

Macquarie not only sought to instill a greater sense of law and order; he also sought to make sure that this sense of law and order was applied to everyone evenly. Macquarie was not given to favoritism and openly embraced the full rehabilitation of the convict classes in the colony that he governed. He still used convict labor, though, as was evident in the major projects that established towns such as Bathurst and Penrith. Even so, Macquarie provided these workers with some kind of light at the end of the tunnel. He even paved the way for emancipated convicts to be given the right to purchase land of their own.

As one might imagine, the Exclusive class did not necessarily appreciate these inroads made by the former convicts. Still, Macquarie's tenure as governor seems to have been a stunning success. Under Macquarie, the colony expanded both territorially and economically. Governor-General Macquarie kickstarted huge public works projects, which built up colonial infrastructure. Notable buildings and bridges were built, and roads spiraled out from the growing capital of Sydney to the surrounding satellite settlements.

During Macquarie's time as governor, the population greatly increased. At the start of his administration, the population was around 11,590, and it is believed to have been around 38,778 toward the end of his tenure. These efforts would lead to Macquarie later being hailed as the Father of Australia.

However, this supposed founding father was not always popular with his peers, and the Exclusives, in particular, did not appreciate Macquarie's methods. His outreach to former convicts had the more affluent Australians, led by John Thomas Bigge, calling for his removal, which led to his dismissal in 1821. Macquarie was replaced by Sir Thomas Brisbane, who served as the sixth governor-general of New South Wales.

During Brisbane's time as governor, the settlements in Australia were given full colonial status, which came with all of the rights the British

Crown granted to lands with such status. Additionally, the island of Tasmania during this period was, for the first time, recognized as its own separate territory. It was now seen as being separate from the mainland.

Brisbane embarked on a decidedly less tolerant approach to the Aboriginals. His aggressive push against the local inhabitants would soon be keenly felt by them. This was especially true as it pertained to Tasmania, for in 1825, Brisbane launched the Black War.

This war was nothing short of an effort to push an entire ethnicity (hence the reference to "black" Aboriginals) from their ancestral lands. Brisbane established a clear dividing line between the colonial settlements and the Natives of Tasmania and then continued to push this line farther and farther south. Eventually, the Aboriginals of Tasmania were pushed off the island and relocated to nearby Flinders Island, which was established as a reservation for them. Despite all of these efforts, modern Tasmanian residents cite Aboriginal heritage, demonstrating that some remained and even intermarried with colonialists. It is believed that just over 5 percent of the Tasmanian population today identify as being of Aboriginal descent.

Although the main tactic was blatant aggression against the Aboriginal people, there were some people who took a much softer approach. Captain George Grey, who was operating out of western Australia in 1840, came to view the Aboriginals rather fondly. Even though the Aboriginals did not adhere to what was then considered modern society at the time, he felt they were very smart and quick-witted. He also considered the possibilities of what could be accomplished if colonists worked with these intelligent and capable people instead of working against them.

Captain George Grey and others like him embarked on efforts to supposedly "civilize" the Aboriginal people so they could be more readily absorbed into the rest of colonial society. It was believed that the biggest hurdle behind good relations between settlers and Aboriginals was the fact that Aboriginals lived a very unsettled life. They were wandering nomads and hunter-gatherers by nature, so it was believed that if they were taught to settle down in one place and learn how to farm, colonial society could more easily relate to them.

Getting the Aboriginal people to settle on one stable plot of land was the first step. But they also had to get the Aboriginals to wear Western-styled clothes, learn how to read and write, and convert to Christianity.

This was the dream that many of these more soft-hearted colonialists had. Many today would condemn the motivations and aspirations of these so-called "civilizers." However, these colonizers obviously felt that they were serving a good cause. Unlike those who aggressively brushed the Indigenous people aside, these people were making an effort to integrate the Aboriginal people into colonial society so there could be peace.

One of those who sincerely believed in these efforts of social, cultural, and religious conversion was Reverend Robert Cartwright, who served as a chaplain in the colony in 1820. Cartwright was later quoted to have said of this social experiment that the locals would "be completely weaned from [their] roving habits."[i]

Children were seen as the number one targets of this indoctrination. It was believed that teaching the younger generations was crucial for creating any real and meaningful change in Aboriginal society. It was thought that if the children could be taught and raised in Western ways, they would then teach their parents. Even more importantly, they would teach the generations after them, creating a lasting generational shift among the Indigenous population.

This decision to make a comprehensive outreach to youngsters would essentially lead to efforts to systematically brainwash Aboriginal children. In some cases, kids would practically be kidnapped to live at private institutions set up specifically for the task of indoctrinating them. The memory of this forced indoctrination would lead to lasting scars on later generations of the Aboriginal people of Australia.

The efforts indeed led to a generational and cultural shift, just not exactly the kind that those who perpetuated it had sought. The vacuum left by these stolen generations is one of the saddest legacies and lingering effects of colonization in Australia.

The efforts to educate Aboriginals in Western ways were fleeting at best. Some children did take to the education that was provided, but they were few in number. Most Aboriginal children ran from the school and were never seen again. In other words, there was no consistency in these efforts, so no real progress was made.

---

[i] Blainey, Geoffrey. *A Shorter History of Australia*. 1994. Pg. 43.

However, the depredations and encroachment on tribal lands were consistent and steadily eroded away what was left of the Aboriginal way of life. Most pressing was the growing number of sheep farms. As mentioned earlier, once the colonists got the hang of what type of sheep to use and how to raise them, sheep farming became a very profitable business in Australia. By the mid-19th century, sheep farms had grown exponentially. These farmers took up a lot of land, and much of that land was the traditional hunting grounds of the Aboriginals. The Aboriginals were no longer able to hunt and gather on their own as they had in the past, so they became increasingly dependent on the colonists. They depended on handouts of supplies, such as flour, sugar, and the like, and worked odd jobs for colonial taskmasters. There was indeed a generational shift in the works for Aboriginal society and their traditional ways of life, but it certainly did not seem to be one for the better.

Chapter 4: Gold Rush and Economic Boom: The Transformative 19th Century

"Land where gaunt and haggard women live alone and work like men. Till their husbands, gone a-droving, will return to them again."
-Henry Lawson[1]

Since at least the early 1800s, gold had been known to exist in various parts of the Australian colony of New South Wales. In 1815, inmates consigned to building the Great Western Road discovered many small gold deposits. Additional discoveries of gold deposits were made in the 1820s and 1830s.

However, all of these finds were in small quantities. Even so, the locations were largely kept quiet by those in charge, just in case they might produce better results later on.

The real breakthrough moment for Australia's gold rush is actually related to the gold rush in the US territory of California in 1849. (The gold rush of 1849 would later lend its name to an NFL football team, the San Francisco 49ers.) The California Gold Rush is a classic tale of fortune, greed, and opportunity. But what does it have to do with Australia? The connection lies in a British-Australian transplant who

---

[1] Macintyre, Stuart. A Concise History of Australia. 1999. Pg. 98.

spent some time in California during the gold rush of 1849. His name was Edward Hargraves, and he was marginally successful in mining gold in California.

His real "eureka" moment came when he realized that the lands in California that contained gold looked strikingly similar to the land he had seen in New South Wales. Hargraves returned to Australia in January of 1851 and teamed up with another gold prospector, John Lister. Together, they forged a prodigious prospecting operation, which managed to strike gold in a location called Lewis Ponds Creek.

A painting of Hargraves.[9]

The expedition broke down when terrible infighting took place over just who would take credit for the finds. Some scholars have since argued that Hargraves and Lister's role in the gold rush was overblown, but shortly after their efforts began, a motivation to find gold in Australia seemed to take hold. It has been estimated that during the rest of the 1850s, Australian mining managed to dredge up some one thousand tons of gold. This new influx of gold made up around 40 percent of the global total production of the precious metal before the decade was out.

This gold boom went hand in hand with a population boom, with the Australian population reaching one million for the first time in the year 1861.

As one might imagine, the gold rush brought about some rather far-reaching socioeconomic changes. The most obvious change was the population's rapid transition from farming communities to mining towns. Due to this rapid shift, the previously booming wheat production of the Australian colonies fell considerably. In Victoria alone, it is believed that production dropped by 75 percent in the first couple of years of the gold rush. Sheep were left untended, and farms went unplowed as the average Australian sought to make it rich digging gold rather than digging ditches. As a direct result, the price of food went through the roof. Wheat products, potatoes, cabbage, and eggs became exceedingly expensive.

The very last ship of convict settlers, the Hougoumont, arrived in Western Australia on January 9th, 1868. This marked the official end of Britain's practice of transporting criminals to Australia, closing a chapter that had lasted eighty years. By this time, free settlers had come to outnumber convicts and their descendants, as waves of gold miners and immigrants had poured into the continent during the mid-19th century.

Most former convicts, whose sentences had long since been completed, quietly lived out their lives in settlements across Australia. It is likely that some even lived into the early 20th century, with writer and historian Geoffrey Blainey suggesting that a few hardy souls may have still been alive at the outbreak of World War II in 1939. While no official records confirm this, it remains an intriguing possibility, though many ex-convicts were reluctant to speak of their past due to the stigma.

It is also quite likely that some of these former convicts took to the goldfields, seeking fortune and a fresh start during the gold rush era of the 1850s and 1860s.

The mining towns and the towns near gold mines were rapidly overwhelmed by wave after wave of gold-seeking migrants. It was not likely that anyone was checking the backgrounds of these gold miners to see who had past convictions. Ironically enough, many of these gold miners had already tried their luck in California, only to become discouraged by what was perceived as the lawless nature of the gold mines and mining towns. According to historian and scholar Barbara West, these intrepid souls had flocked to Australia in order to take advantage of its well-established British laws and customs.

Not everyone benefited from these so-called British customs, though. Many miners arrived from China, and they had a rough go of things, especially when compared to their mining counterparts. Eventually, laws were even passed to restrict Chinese involvement in mining. Heavy taxes were levied against ships carrying Chinese migrants. Some Chinese found a way around this by showing up far from the goldfields in southern Australia, where there was no landing tax levied on the ships that carried them. However, they still had to get to the gold mines, which meant they were in for a long and dangerous overland walk.[i]

Hostile miners frequently harassed the Chinese who managed to reach the Australian goldfields. Tensions between European and Australian miners and the Chinese often ran high. Resentment toward the Chinese boiled over in June 1861 when one of the most violent anti-Chinese riots in Australian history erupted: the Lambing Flat riots.

The riot broke out after a bill to restrict Chinese miners failed to pass. Fueled by anger and jealousy, thousands of White miners descended on a Chinese mining camp and attacked its residents. Many Chinese miners were violently beaten, their camps burned, and their belongings destroyed. Some were even scalped by the rioters, while others fled into the nearby bush.

Authorities eventually stepped in, sending police and military forces to restore order. Though some of the main agitators were arrested, none were executed, and many escaped serious punishment altogether. Despite the violence, some Chinese miners returned to the goldfields, determined to continue their work.

One of the more interesting and consequential developments of the gold rush was the decision to phase out the previous convict system of immigration. Such a change had been in the works for a while. Back in Britain, the notion that convicted criminals were being sent to lands filled with gold, which could lead those convicts to either eventually strike it

---

[i] Blainey, Geoffrey. *A Shorter History of Australia*. 1994. Pg. 71.

rich or rob someone else of their riches, began to seem a bit ridiculous to the powers that be. It was determined that the time was ripe to begin the process of phasing out the old system of convict settlers. In December 1852, the British government officially ended all transportation of convicts to the Australian east coast.

By this time, the convicts had already made quite an impact on the culture of Australia. In fact, the legacy of escaped convicts gave rise to the infamous bushrangers. The term was originally used to refer to escaped convicts who hid in the wilderness of the Australian Outback. These escapees often used armed robberies as a means to sustain themselves as they roamed around the range. The term bushranger stuck, and later on, almost any habitual armed robbing gang was referred to as bushrangers. The Ned Kelly gang was among the most infamous (we will talk about him more in the next chapter).

This decade of the gold rush saw the passage of the landmark Australian Colonies Government Act in 1850. This act granted Van Diemen's Land (better known as Tasmania), South Australia, and the colony of Victoria their own legislative councils and allowed for a limited form of representative government.

Because of the gold rush, the emancipation of convicts, and this newfound representation, the Australian colonies experienced a veritable population boom. It is believed that during this period, the population of Australia rose from around 430,000 in 1851 to over one million by 1861. Victoria became the biggest and most heavily populated colony, and Melbourne became the biggest city. Interestingly, Melbourne was also a leader in printed news media, with *The Age* coming to prominence as a popular periodical printed on Australia's newly minted steam-powered printing press. This paper kept Australians up on all of the latest happenings, both near and far. By 1890, it is said to have been regularly selling over 100,000 editions a day, cementing its place as one of the leading papers of the day.

So, the gold rush ultimately led to a population boom and an information explosion. The newly christened railroads and trains helped to carry this information. These stretches of railroad would come to cover much of Australia, and they first began in the city of Melbourne.

The landing at Melbourne in 1840.[10]

All of these things helped to create the perfect backdrop for the noteworthy events to come.

Chapter 5: The Push Inland, Federation, and the Birth of Australia

"The night too quickly passes. And we are growing old. So let us fill our glasses. And toast the Days of Gold. When finds of wondrous treasure, set all the south ablaze. And you and I were faithful mates. All through the roaring days."

-Henry Lawson[1]

From November 1859 to January 1860, a special committee belonging to the Philosophical Institute of Victoria (which would later be renamed the Royal Society) looked into the possibility of exploring the mostly unexplored interior of the Australian Outback. Up until that point, Australia's settlements had mostly been coastal ones. These bold and inquisitive explorers of the committee viewed it as their responsibility—and the responsibility of Queen Victoria's Britain—to push forward into the unknown. Yes, almost like the opening monologue of *Star Trek*, these Australian settlers felt it was their duty to boldly go where no Brit had gone before.

Queen Victoria's namesake colony, the bustling Australian outpost of Victoria, would lead the charge. Victoria was the richest of the Australian

---

[1] Macintyre, Stuart. A Concise History of Australia. 1999. Pg. 90.

colonies, and it was believed that it was in a prime position to move farther into the Australian interior. This push galvanized the younger generation of Australians. They saw the push into the interior as a push forward for society and civilization in general.

The committee was chaired by Sir William Stawell, who was the Chief Justice of Victoria Supreme Court. The committee members were considered to be refined gentlemen in the traditional British sense of the term. This meant that the leaders of the expedition into the Australian interior were basically from the noble classes of the Anglo-Australian strata, while their subordinates were made up of the lower classes. Those who worked under the leaders of these expeditions ranged from the poor to former convicts to perhaps even a small number of Aboriginals. The latter would have served largely as guides and translators.

Among the leaders of the group were also scientists, such as the esteemed John Macadam, who was a chemist by trade, and Ferdinand von Mueller, who held a PhD in botany. Von Mueller was renowned for his ability to identify and categorize unique flora and fauna in Australia.

Those who headed this expedition placed great trust in recent advances in both communication and transportation. These innovations aided their progress as they pushed farther inland, venturing into harsh and uncharted territories. One notable advancement was the expansion of the overland telegraph, which laid the foundation for faster and more reliable communication between remote regions. The introduction of camel transport, first brought to Australia in the 1860s, also proved invaluable for crossing the arid interior, allowing explorers to carry more supplies over longer distances.

There was also a religious motivation. As Australian historian and writer Manning Clark put it, many Australians felt as if they were somehow being singled out by God to bring about what they viewed as the Christian (at least the Westernized variation) way of life. Surveyor John McDouall Stuart was one of those who firmly believed in this supposed mission. John first attempted an expedition to the Australian interior in November 1859. This mission was largely a bust, and he and his team quickly retreated back to the colonial settlements.

Not to be deterred, Stuart and company made another attempt in March 1860. This time around, they were much more successful and managed to reach the mid-point of the Australian Outback. Here, he and his team raised the British flag. The Union Jack was stuck in a large mound of land that would later be dubbed Central Mount Stuart. The team then traveled another 150 miles northwest before sickness and hunger forced them to turn back.

Another expedition would be launched that fall with the purpose of traveling all the way across the Australian continent. This expedition led by explorers, Robert O'Hara Burke and William John Willis, successfully crossed in a south-north direction, from Melbourne to the Gulf of Carpentaria. Burke and company learned some things along the way from the locals they encountered, including the consumption of a desert plant called nardoo. They had witnessed the locals preparing the stuff and were intrigued. It seemed good enough to them, so the hungry explorers decided to add it to their diet.

Unfortunately for them, they failed to properly roast the plant before grinding it down for consumption, leading to some rather dire results. The nardoo plant has a thiamine (vitamin B1) blocker, which can lead to starvation. The men were puzzled to find that no matter how much nardoo or any other foodstuff they consumed, they were getting skinnier and skinnier. Their bodies were actually being overloaded by thiamine blockers, so they were no longer able to absorb nutrients. Burke and Willis both perished as a result.

This expedition would be followed by another in 1862. It was led by John McDouall Stuart, who helped to map out a large section of the Australian interior. This proved to be crucial for the placing of a telegraph line (the Australian Overland Telegraph Line), which would travel hundreds of miles across Australia. Another milestone was achieved by explorer Ernest Giles, who blazed a path from Adelaide to Perth in 1875.

While Australian explorers were making great inroads across the interior of Australia, the so-called "bushrangers" began to cause trouble in the more established regions. The trouble with the bushrangers had already been brewing before the 1860s, but it escalated following the introduction of the Selection Acts. These acts aimed to break up large squatter-owned landholdings and open up Crown land for purchase by small farmers.

An image of bushrangers.[11]

Two of the most significant acts were the 1861 Crown Lands Alienation Act and the 1861 Crown Lands Occupation Act in New South Wales. Under these laws, settlers—known as "selectors"—could purchase between 40 and 640 acres at one pound per acre, with 20 percent due upfront and the remainder payable over three years.

Other Australian colonies followed suit. Victoria introduced the Duffy Act in 1862, Queensland passed its own Selection Act in 1868, and South Australia followed with the Strangways Act in 1869. These laws encouraged small-scale farming, but they also led to bitter conflicts between selectors and wealthy squatters, who often tried to drive them off the land.

When land prospectors began to utilize loopholes in the ruling to purchase and create monopolies on land holdings, the poor classes began to suffer. They were not only in debt, but they also found themselves the owners of rather unproductive tracts of land in inhospitable environments. The children of these poor farmers often grew up to become desperadoes. The disparities led to resentment, and soon, the perceived freedom of "the bush" came calling. Poor bands of robbers sought to play Robin Hood by imitating the ex-convict bushrangers of the past. The bushranger gangs roamed the wild bushlands, living on the plunder they accumulated. The most famous of these bushranger gangs to rise to prominence was the Ned Kelly gang. Although Ned has become a popular anti-hero of sorts, historian Manning Clark did not pull any punches in his description of him. In his blunt assessment, he stated, "Ned Kelly was a wild ass of a man, snarling, roaring and frothing like a ferocious beast when the tamer entered the cage."[i]

Considering all of the damage he caused, such snap judgments are easy to make. But to be fair, if one simply looked into Ned Kelly's upbringing, it becomes much easier to understand how he ended up the way he did. Ned's dad was sent to Australia from Ireland in 1843 as part of his punishment for stealing a couple of pigs. Shortly after his arrival, he met Ned's mother, Ellen Quinn, who gave birth to Ned in June 1855.

Seemingly doomed from day one, Ned was born with the stigma of being the child of a convict. Ned was raised to distrust authority figures, with his father repeatedly complaining about how those of an Irish background, such as himself, could never expect to get a fair trial at the hands of British authorities.

Ned Kelly's father died in 1866, and his father's passing led that cumbersome chip on Ned's shoulder to only get bigger. His widowed mother took him and his siblings to live on a small plot of land situated at a place called Eleven Mile Creek, which was located somewhere in the middle of the settlements of Glenrowan and Greta.

This section of Australia was a real no man's land back in those days, and many rough and rugged bushrangers passed through. These men greatly influenced Ned, and soon, he was picking up their habits. He became a skilled horse thief early on, learning the art of ambushing unwary travelers.

However, his activities soon got the attention of the police. In 1870, he was arrested by Constable Thomas Lonigan. It is said that Lonigan was pretty rough with Ned and actually dragged him across the ground in the process of taking him into custody.

Several years later, in 1878, matters truly came to a head. On April 15th, 1878, an incident occurred that changed the trajectory of the lives of Ned's whole family. It was on that day that the police arrived at the Kelly homestead with a warrant to arrest one of Ned's brothers for stealing a horse. Constable Fitzpatrick fully expected to take the young man into custody with little to no issue. However, the arresting officer was met by the angry Kelly mother swinging a shovel. Someone from the house fired off a shot, which managed to hit Fitzpatrick in his wrist. The officer was

---

[i] Clark, Manning. *A History of Australia*. 1988.

probably lucky that the Kelly gang did not finish him off then and there. They obviously could have fired a finishing shot, and Ned's mother was right there with a shovel to bury the evidence.

Although they let the officer leave, Ned Kelly warned him not to speak a word of the incident to a soul. Ned must have greatly overestimated his powers of intimidation. If he expected a police officer with a bullet lodged in his wrist to simply forget all about his warrant and tell the folks down at the police station that everything was just fine, he had gravely misunderstood the situation.

The officer reported everything that had occurred, and an arrest warrant was put out for his mother, the shovel-wielding Ellen Kelly. She was taken into police custody while Ned fled to the safety of the bush. From his refuge, he would strike back at the police in a most devastating manner.

Ned Kelly came upon an encampment of police officers on October 26th, 1878, and shot and killed three of them. A fourth man—Constable McIntyre—managed to get away. McIntyre told the rest of the police department about what had happened.

The police were outraged. To see their own officers gunned down was bad enough, but the fact that this gang of bushrangers seemed determined to continually flout the law and live by their own rules was deemed intolerable as it pertained to civil society. Ned and his gang were not just criminals at this point; they were insurrectionist revolutionaries who defied all rules and were attempting to set up their own form of government.

As was the case with Ned Kelly, these bushranger gangs were in constant battles with the police. According to historian Manning Clark, during this period, at least eleven policemen were murdered, and many more were wounded just trying to bring some of these

Ned Kelly the day before his execution.[13]

criminals to justice. Yes, despite some of the later romanticism attached to bushrangers like Ned Kelly, it must be remembered that they were criminals and that their actions led to death and destruction.

Furthermore, the society that so many had been trying to establish in Australia would not survive if such lawlessness was left unchecked. The Australian colonial powers had to either confront and put an end to the bushrangers; if they did not, Australia could devolve into a seething cesspool of chaos and corruption.

Many bushrangers seemed to prefer chaos over an orderly society any day of the week. One infamous bushranger, Ben Hall, terrorized Australia from 1863 to 1865. He went on a rampage of robbing, killing, and destruction that brought Australian civil society to its knees. He was the son of former Australian convicts and seemed to live up to the hellion stereotype of the later bushrangers. As historian Manning Clark described him, "Hall had a private hell in his heart against society in general and the police in particular."[1]

Bushrangers like Hall despised authority and especially hated the police, as was evidenced by the frequent shootouts they had with the cops during the course of their many exploits. Ben Hall was left dead after coming out on the losing end of one of these exchanges. His corpse was found riddled with bullets in May 1865. He was only twenty-seven years old when he was killed.

Ned Kelly met a similar—if perhaps more infamous—fate. Prior to his final showdown, Ned Kelly had been planning one of his boldest and deadliest robberies yet. His plan? To derail and ambush a police train near Glenrowan, Victoria. In preparing for the attack, he and his gang took over the town, holding dozens of locals hostage at the Glenrowan Inn.

As fate would have it, one of those who managed to escape—local schoolteacher Thomas Curnow—would become Kelly's undoing. Curnow convinced the gang to let him leave, claiming he needed to care for his ill wife and child. Ned might have thought he was showing some measure of kindness, but if so, it was the last kind act he would make.

Once freed, Curnow placed a lantern on the railway tracks and frantically signaled the oncoming police train, warning them of the trap

---

[1] Clark, Manning. *A History of Australia*. 1988.

ahead. Instead of blindsiding an unprepared police force, the Kelly gang was the ones being ambushed.

Heavily armed police swarmed the Glenrowan Inn, and an all-night siege began. The building was riddled with bullets; over fifteen thousand rounds were fired. By morning, Ned Kelly, clad in his makeshift armor, emerged from the smoke and gunfire for one final stand. But the police brought him down with shots to his unprotected legs, ending the reign of Australia's most infamous bushranger.[i]

The police leaped upon the armored figure writhing on the ground in agony. Ned reportedly accepted defeat and was placed under police custody without any further incident. His subsequent trial became something of a sensation in Australia, and many still tended to view him sympathetically despite his crimes. Nevertheless, he was found guilty, and on November 11th, 1880, he was executed.

In many ways, as Australian "civilized" society moved farther into the Australian interior, it was those at the margins of society—the bushrangers—who stood up as the last real, formidable impediment of this forward motion of civilization. Many also began to realize that the Selection Acts, which had monopolized land holdings, contributed to the problem of landless rogues turning to a life of crime. This was noted in a local Australian paper called the *Empire* in an article first printed on February 11th, 1867. The article stated, "The end of the present system of land monopoly will involve the end of bushranging. Whenever the interior wilderness is thrown fully open to the industrious cultivator of the soil—when families are allowed to make permanent homes—then and not till then will the bushranging brood be extirpated."[ii] Soon enough, it was clear to most Australians that in order to bring about a much-needed change of heart among the lower classes, there would need to be a change in the system of government itself.

In March of 1891, tidings from Queensland, a settlement on the northeastern coast of Australia, were beginning to concern the Australian powers that be. In this part of colonial Australia, disaffected laborers were going on strike, and in one incident, they even burned down several woolsheds in Lorne and Mangroo. Woolsheds were where traditional wool shearers cut wool from sheep.

---

[i] West, Barbara A. *A Brief History of Australia*. 2010. Pg. 70.

[ii] Clark, Manning. *A History of Australia*. 1988. Pg. 311.

Those responsible for shearing all of those sheep were not happy with labor conditions. There were the typical complaints of long hours and low pay, but these laborers were also upset with new methodologies that had been introduced. In particular, they took umbrage at the introduction of new fencing that included barbed wire and made the old-fashioned method of sheep shepherding obsolete. They were also frustrated with new machines that were being introduced that threatened to make the job of shearing sheep by hand not even necessary.

At this time, the demand for wool had increased considerably, and the profits of the companies behind this enterprise were increasing. Yet, the people who sheared these sheep felt they were being denied their benefits and even being phased out altogether.

These sheep shearers were indeed upset, and they wanted everyone to know about it. The shearers even went as far as to set the surrounding grasslands ablaze.

At this point, the line between passionate political protest and outright rebellion seemed blurred. Fearing an escalation, Queensland authorities sent in armed police and military forces to restore order. Yet, the wet season's torrential rains turned the roads into muddy, impassable terrain, making it nearly impossible for the authorities to track down the striking shearers.

This emboldened the strikers, who refused to back down. Their demands grew beyond wages and working conditions, with some pushing for greater political representation for workers. However, their fight was soon cut short. In March 1891, police arrested strike leaders, charging them with sedition and conspiracy. The strike was effectively crushed.

While the strike failed, the battle for workers' rights continued at the ballot box. That same year, the Australian Labor Party (ALP) was formed, marking the first time a political party was founded with the working class at its core. Across the colonies, Labor candidates began winning seats. Among them was Adolphus George Taylor, a firebrand politician known for his populist speeches and advocacy for workers' rights. Though not a direct leader of the Labor movement, his rhetoric captured the frustrations of the working class at a time of great change in Australia's political landscape.

Initially, representatives like Taylor focused solely on uniting the working class, but these efforts eventually morphed into uniting the colonies of Australia. The idea of creating a federation of Australian states was viewed as simply the most logical way to unite the native-born European and largely working-class Australians. Unification was viewed as a means of leveraging more power over the often British-born landed elites and company owners, who lorded over the rest of the Australian populace.

By 1890, the idea of a federation was gaining serious momentum. The six colonies—Western Australia, South Australia, Tasmania, Victoria, New South Wales, and Queensland—seemed ripe for unification.

This push for a federation had its early roots in the Federal Council of Australasia, which was formed in 1885 as a representative body for the Australian colonies. However, the council had limited powers, and New South Wales refused to join, believing a stronger national government was needed.

In 1890, colonial representatives met in Melbourne to formally discuss the prospect of a federation. While no immediate decisions were made, the conference paved the way for the 1891 Constitutional Convention in Sydney.

Sir Henry Parkes delivering the first resolution at the federation conference in Melbourne in March 1890.[18]

At this 1891 convention, delegates—including key figures such as Sir Samuel Griffith, Edmund Barton, and Henry Parkes—drafted the first version of the Australian Constitution. However, political divisions and a lack of public support at the time meant the effort stalled. It would take nearly a decade of debating and campaigning before a federation finally became a reality in 1901.

In 1893, another constitutional convention was held. The convention met in the city of Corowa and discussed steps to have elected delegates participate in a referendum across the colonies to endorse a federal constitution. This became known as the Corowa Plan.

More conventions were held in 1897 and 1898, which moved things along even further. A plan had been put forward to establish a constitutional commonwealth of federated Australian states that would still (at least ostensibly) be under the British Crown. In March 1900, delegates were sent to London to get an official federation bill passed. This bill was finally passed on July 5th, 1900, and approved on July 9th. This led to the official declaration of the Commonwealth of Australia on January 1st, 1901.

Chapter 6: World War I and Australia's Increasing Role in Global Conflicts

"Our wounded are most amazing. They sing, they cheer, they smoke their cigarettes."

-General Sir John Monash

Just prior to the outbreak of the First World War, the British Empire was at its height, and the average Australian was receiving all of the benefits of its imperial largesse. Even though Australia had become a federation, it was still linked at the hip with Britain. British ideas, goods, and migrants continued to flow freely into Australia. Even as late as 1914, many government positions in Australia were still being taken up by people who had been born in Britain. In 1914, the Australian governor-general was British-born.

Considering as much, when the First World War erupted that very year, it was no surprise that Australia was ready to rally the troops for what was ostensibly a British cause in the fight over hegemony in Europe. This was not the first time that assistance from Australia was expected. During the Second Boer War (1899-1902), Australia delivered military support when British interests in South Africa were

---

[1] Blainey, Geoffrey. *A Shorter History of Australia*. 1994. Pg. 158.

threatened.

In order to explain how the Australians became involved in the Boer War, some background is necessary. The Portuguese were the first to make landfall on South Africa's Cape of Good Hope when they circumnavigated the tip of Africa in the late 15th century. The Portuguese originally called it the Cape of Storms due to the turbulent weather conditions often found there. The name was quickly changed to Cabo da Boa Esperança, which translates to "Cape of Good Hope." This name change came about due to the renewed sense of optimism and hope that the circumnavigation of Africa had brought. The Portuguese had now found an alternative route to India and had access to the lucrative Asian trade.

The Portuguese might have been the first Europeans to touch down in the region, but their competitors, the Dutch, were the first to stay. They created a permanent settlement that developed into Cape Town, which then grew into the larger South African settlement of Cape Colony.

The status of the Dutch in the region remained unchanged until the French Revolution brought French troops to the Dutch settlement in 1795. The British, who were battling the French for dominance, arrived right on their heels and seized Cape Colony for themselves. Several years later, the Dutch ended up officially handing the colony over to the British by way of the Anglo-Dutch Treaty of 1814.

But even though the Dutch ceded their territory to the British, many Dutch settlers known as Boers remained. They pushed into frontier country to forge independent settlements during an exodus known as the Great Trek. This resulted in the Dutch-Boer colonies like the Transvaal and the Orange Free State.

However, after some rather lucrative mineral deposits of diamonds and gold were discovered in these regions, the British and Boers began to bump heads, leading to the Boer Wars. With the eruption of the Second Boer War in 1899, many Australian troops were sent to the region to participate in the fighting against the Dutch Boers.

The Australian cavalry units known as lancers played the most pivotal role. These Aussie lancers stormed right into the siege of Kimberley in February 1900. Kimberley was a diamond mining town that had been captured by the Boers, and the Australian lancers helped to break this siege. The Australian troops also played a prominent role in the battles of Paardeberg and Modder River.

The Boers surrendered in May 1902. Britain absorbed the colonies, and in 1910, the region became a self-governing dominion under the British flag. This was all accomplished with the help of their Australian allies.

Back in the days of the Boer Wars, it seemed that British and Australian cooperation was expected. However, as it pertains to World War I, many modern-day historians have expressed surprise at how eager the Australians were to provide military assistance. Part of this eagerness was due to the closely perceived historical and cultural ties between Australia and Britain.

However, there was a more pragmatic reason to support the British as well. The Australians viewed the British as their protectors. The British navy and its ability to project power far and wide kept many possible threats at bay.

Japan had risen up as a world power by this point, and there was great fear that the Japanese might one day threaten Australia. The events of World War II would prove that these fears were not unfounded. There were also other actors in the region that could have turned hostile to Australian interests if the British were not there to enforce the status quo.

The Australians, therefore, very much believed that the defense of Britain was in their own best interest. During World War I, the principal foe—Germany—made inroads in Australia's backyard. The Germans had a colonial outpost in what we now call Papua New Guinea.

The large island just north of Australia is referred to as New Guinea as a whole, and it has a rather complicated history. Just prior to World War I, the island was split up between the French, British, and Germans. The French controlled the western half of the island, the British controlled the southeastern portion, and the Germans controlled the northeastern portion.

After the outbreak of World War I, the German outpost in the northeast of the island became a front line of the war. In the early stages of the conflict, Australian naval units seized Rabaul, a strategic port in German New Guinea. The Australian armed forces also seized the German island of Nauru, seizing control of a German radio station in the process.

Another early incident involved an Australian naval vessel opening fire on a German warcraft called the *Emden*. The German ship was pulverized and made inoperable.

Australia's naval forces proved themselves battle-ready in these early exchanges. This was an important test since Australia's navy was relatively new. It was only in 1909 that Australia's dominion fleet was approved.

After these early naval exchanges in and around Australian territory, the Australian armed forces began to be transferred to take up the fight in Europe and the Middle East. One of Germany's main allies in the war was the Ottoman Empire, whose heart lay in Istanbul (previously Constantinople), Turkey. The British were eager to open up a front here. The goal was to knock the Turks out of the war and open up a supply line over the Black Sea to nearby Russia, which was fighting on the side of the Allies.

The Russians were already faltering at this point due to domestic problems, and they were in dire need of supplies. The Russians had a massive army but were often seriously lacking in equipment. There were even instances in which threadbare Russian troops faced off against their foes barefoot. Britain and France hoped to provide proper equipment to their Russian ally, lest the Germans, who were tearing through the Eastern Front, brought the Russians to their knees.

This was all part of the Gallipoli campaign. This campaign was named after the narrow strip of land that reaches across the Dardanelles to the Turkish mainland, where British and Australian troops had landed. The British war planners seemed to think that marching along this narrow peninsula would be easy, but it was not. In fact, it was a horrendous nightmare. The troops were squeezed into very narrow, close quarters and had to battle their way through intense and determined machine gun fire.

During this struggle, the Australians were part of a special group of fighters that included troops from neighboring New Zealand. The contingent was dubbed the Australian and New Zealand Army Corps, or "ANZAC" for short. It is said that around eight thousand Australians were killed in this melee.

After about eight months, the British high command was mortified to have to order a withdrawal. It was deemed too hard and too costly to continue the mission. The last Australian troops evacuated this death trap just a few days before Christmas in 1915.

Nevertheless, many Australians viewed this unmitigated disaster as a baptism of fire that brought them onto the world stage as serious participants in international affairs. Even though the mission was a failure, the brave Australians who were willing to sacrifice their lives would be forever remembered on ANZAC Day. This is an officially designated national holiday in Australia that is celebrated on April 25th. Although the holiday began in remembrance of those who fought and died during this doomed military operation in World War I, it later became a memorial day that celebrated those who had served or died in wars.

After the failed Gallipoli campaign, many Australians began to be sent in large numbers to France, the Western Front of the war. They soon found themselves fighting trench warfare, which was just about as brutal and static as what they had faced in Turkey. Soldiers from all of the Allied countries were dying at an appalling rate.

It was soon decided that a rapid recruitment drive was needed. There just were not enough soldiers to fight on the Western Front. Australia was tapped to send even more soldiers. This led W. M. Hughes, the Labor prime minister, to start a draft of army-age men so that they could be sent to France. The decision became an unpopular one as the war continued, and in November 1916, the Labor Party faced consequences at the ballot box.

Voters were upset because of the draft and the economic toll that the war was taking on life back home in Australia. Both the cost of food and the price of rent had gone up considerably, significantly affecting working-class Australians. By 1917, most Australians were feeling the bite of inflation. Meanwhile, the political elites continued to try to sell their war aims.

Australians in Egypt in 1914. The kangaroo was their mascot.[14]

Nevertheless, the war dragged on, and in 1917, Australian troops took part in the epic Battle of Gaza. The Levant, a region home to modern-day nation-states and territories such as Israel and Palestine, was still under the dominion of the Ottoman Empire at that time. The British and their Australian allies duked it out with the Turks here as well.

As successful as the Turks were at defending the Turkish homeland, they could not defend this territory too terribly well. The British and their allies won the day here, and the whole region became a British mandate. Eventually, it would be carved up into the nations and territories we have come to recognize today. Of course, the history of the Middle East is much more complicated than that simple summary, and ownership of these lands has changed many times over the past few thousand years or so.

World War I would come to a close on November 11th, 1918, when the defeated Germans signed an armistice. Australian troops did not participate in the Allied occupation of Germany since Australian Prime Minister Hughes felt it was in the nation's best interest to return their fighting men back to Australia as soon as possible.

Upon their return, they were met by many Australians who had some rather ambivalent feelings about the war. Additionally, many of these troops were not exactly in a celebratory mood. Why did they fight? Just to support Britain? Although the fight was argued to be in Australia's best interest, many in the public failed to see it.

Even worse, the war had been a costly one for Australia. There were even difficulties coming up with the finances to dole out the pensions expected from all of the returning soldiers, many of whom had been rendered permanently disabled. Others faced chronic nervous conditions, which back then would have been referred to as shell shock. This disorder was called as such because it was felt that the shock of hearing the blasting of artillery shells and other loud explosions over a long, sustained period created an acute nervous condition in soldiers. Now, we are more likely to refer to such a distressed state as being PTSD or post-traumatic stress disorder.

To treat these distressed veterans, the Returned Services League, or RSL, was put in place. First established in 1916 while the war was still raging, the RSL spearheaded special programs and facilities to aid veterans who had just returned from the front.

Australian politicians often spoke of crafting legislation that would make Australia a land fit for heroes. In many ways, though, this idyllic postwar vision failed to come to fruition. Most glaring is the fact that Aboriginal veterans were not even eligible to participate in any of the programs designed for veterans of the First World War. They were denied any further medical care and not allowed to take part in a special soldier resettlement program that gave returning Australian servicemen of European ancestry land to settle. This was indeed unsettling since many Indigenous Australians had agreed to take up Australia's fight in order to gain more rights for their people. Instead, they returned home to face more of the same poor treatment.

Nevertheless, for many who had traveled far and wide fighting under the banner of Australia, a fire had been lit within them. During the interwar period between World War I and World War II, the quest for equal rights and a more inclusive Australian society began to take shape.

Chapter 7: The Interwar Period, Aboriginal Rights, and a Stolen Generation

It is estimated that out of the 324,000 some Australians who took part in the war to end all wars (World War I), around 60,000 were killed, and around 150,000 suffered significant injuries. Despite this high toll, the war had some positive outcomes for Australia. The war brought more mobility for the average working-class Australian. It became easier for them to attain high positions in the military and government administration, positions that were not normally open to them.

Even so, these Australians were outliers. Unemployment became a real problem in the immediate postwar period. By 1921, unemployment had risen to as much as 13 percent. Australia was also lagging behind the times compared to much of the rest of the industrialized world as it pertained to items of modern convenience.

In the early 1920s, Britain and the United States were enjoying automobiles, radios, telephones, and the like. Meanwhile, Australians were not quite so privileged. By and large, Australians were still cooking with wood stoves, and firewood was the primary means of keeping warm. Food was more likely to be stored underground in cellars, and the modern convenience of the refrigerator was still largely unknown.

The same could be said for the new-fangled washers and dryers. Australians were still washing and drying their garments by hand. In fact,

Monday was widely known as "washing day" all across Australia. This was the day that clothes could be seen hanging from clotheslines in just about every Australian yard.

Most Australian homes also lacked phones. The phone was seen as more of a fixture for an upscale office than an actual mainstay for the home. The reason behind this perceived backwardness was due to a combination of factors. For one thing, Australia was, in many ways, still considered a far-flung, remote outpost. This was before the days of regular passenger airliners. Travel to Australia was largely relegated to boats, which had to spend months traveling across the high seas. As such, it was much harder for Australia to stay on top of the latest innovations and trends.

However, as much as these descendants of Australia's European colonizers might have lagged behind their industrialized peers, this perceived gap was nothing compared to what the Aboriginal descendants faced. Having lived long on the fringes of Australian colonial society, the Aboriginals had been pushed to the side. Many were grouped together on so-called "mission settlements," which historian Stuart Macintyre described as a process that made them veritable wards of the state.

Even worse was the practice of taking Aboriginal children away from their parents in order to educate them in the ways of "civilized" society. It was believed that the new generations of Aboriginals could be taught to forget about their past and trained for integration into the larger society. It was believed that as these new generations were integrated with the rest of Australia, the mission settlements that looked after the Aboriginals could be dismantled and shut down.

This generation of children, who had been snatched from their parents to be trained in Western ways of thinking, would make up what has been termed the "stolen generation." Many Aboriginal descendants look back on these past actions in horror and describe such things as nothing short of cultural genocide.

During this period, Australian society was not the most receptive to such movements. Australia, just like much of the rest of the world, was rocked by the Great Depression. The Great Depression had started thousands of miles away in the United States when the stock market crashed. Even the most enlightened Australian would have been hard-pressed not to put such lofty notions (at least lofty considering the time period) like Aboriginal rights on the back burner when their own families faced dire deprivation.

Demonstrating just how much the fortunes of countries had become intertwined with each other, this downturn in the United States had ripple effects all across the planet. Times soon became hard in Australia, and by the mid-1930s, the unemployment rate had climbed as high as 21 percent.

Nevertheless, the nascent Aboriginal rights groups began to clamor for more rights. The economic downturn only served as further impetus to take a stand against what had been a long-standing and egregious oppression. They demanded an end to the practice of taking children away from their families and for more inclusion into Australian society.

During this difficult era, Aboriginal groups formed what was eventually called the Aborigines Progressive Association. This group gained widespread attention on January 26th, 1938, for staging the Day of Mourning to commemorate Arthur Phillip's landfall on Australian shores, which kickstarted the forcible displacement of their people. These progressive Aboriginals also called for policy changes that would grant them full citizenship and equality under the Australian government.

The Aboriginals seemed to have reached a sober conclusion. They concluded that they had been done a terrible wrong, but since there was no changing the past, and since the overthrow of the current regime was unlikely, they should at the very least be accorded the same constitutional rights that the descendants of their colonial oppressors enjoyed.

The group did gain the ear of the Australian government, and meetings were even held with the prime minister. The prime minister took their calls for more rights seriously and convened a panel of experts to try to find a better path forward. This panel of experts included everyone from administrators to psychologists to even anthropologists.

Anthropologists suggested that Aboriginal culture should not be suppressed. According to historian Stuart Macintyre, one of these anthropologists, A. P. Elkin, who was a professor of anthropology at the University of Sydney at the time, suggested that Australian administrators should not suppress Aboriginal culture but instead use it as a tool to better the Aboriginals. As Elkin put it, the efforts should be designed to "help them to develop further along their own cultural lines."[i]

These suggestions by Elkin led to calls for an Aboriginal administration that would be informed by anthropological expertise. This new approach was dubbed the "New Deal for Aborigines." The stated aim of this effort was to uplift the Aboriginals and extend to them the ordinary rights of citizenship.

In an article from the popular Melbourne newspaper *The Argus*, dated December 14th, 1938, the basic tenets of this supposed "New Deal" were laid out. Some of the terminology and expressions used are a bit shocking to modern sensibilities since they blatantly categorized Indigenous peoples based on the amount of Indigenous ancestry that flows through their veins. It even makes mention of those who are perceived to be "fully detribalized."

Considering that this was happening during the time of the popular Great Depression-era programs called the New Deal in the United States, spearheaded by Democrat President Franklin Delano Roosevelt, the name is likely not a coincidence. The title seems to suggest great and transformative changes. However, there was nothing really all that progressive about this program as it pertained to the expansion of Aboriginal rights.

On the contrary, it amounted to what Stuart Macintyre described as "extending the practice of forcible removal of Aboriginal children from their families."[ii] The provisions merely sought to categorize those who were considered "detribalized" enough to be snatched up and forcibly "educated" about what was deemed to be proper Australian society.

At this point in Australian history, it seemed that there was a two-pronged approach to the integration of Aboriginal descendants into Australian society. On the one hand, you had a panel of anthropologists headed by Elkin stating that Aboriginal culture should be embraced rather than oppressed, and on the other, you had administrators such as A. O. Neville, who held the rather dubious distinction of being the chief protector of Aboriginals in Western Australia, who insisted that the practice of child removal with the intent of instilling Western values in them was the way forward.

---

[i] Macintyre, Stuart. A Concise History of Australia. 1999.

[ii] Macintyre, Stuart. A Concise History of Australia. 1999.

As much as this debate raged and despite all of the terrible consequences that were brought about, all talk of this matter would get shelved with the outbreak of World War II. The outbreak of the war created an existential threat that seemed to temporarily make these matters moot—the potential invasion of Japan.

Chapter 8: Australia during World War II

"Nothing would come to the men and women of the working class as a gift from the gods. Everything they gained had to be fought for."
    -Australian Prime Minister, John Curtin[i]

The Australian government and its armed forces were pulled into World War II in very much the same way they had been pulled into World War I. Britain had announced its intention to go to war, and Australia, as the most loyal of its allies, followed suit.

Britain had been unsuccessfully trying to avert war by appeasing fascist dictators. Italy's invasion of Ethiopia in 1935 was largely ignored, as was Japan's aggression in China. German aggression in Europe was not entirely ignored, but every trespass was negotiated away. The British under Prime Minister Neville Chamberlain felt they were keeping the peace by appeasing the Germans when they swallowed up the Rhineland, the Sudetenland, Czechoslovakia, and even Austria.

However, when the Germans invaded Poland in September 1939, it was finally considered a bridge too far, and the British, along with their French allies, declared war. After the war was officially declared, Australian Prime Minister Robert Menzies likewise announced that it was his "duty" to let his Australian countrymen know that they, too, were

---
[i] Macintyre, Stuart. A Concise History of Australia. 1999. Pg. 197.

at war with Germany and its allies.

Prime Minister Menzies with Prime Minister Churchill.[15]

Menzies is an iconic character in the history of Australia. He first served as prime minister from 1939 to 1941 before falling out of favor with his political party. Menzies later came back in a big way when he was elected as prime minister again in 1949. He went on to serve until 1966. As of this writing, he is Australia's longest-serving prime minister.

Although Germany was the principal foe in Europe at the outset of World War II, the true menace to Australians was Germany's wartime ally, Japan. Japan had been ramping up its aggression in the region for years and was looking for any excuse to start seizing territory in and around Australia.

The threat to Australia was considerable, but even so, something of a malaise had taken hold of the Australian public when it came to war. Unlike the First World War, which saw young Australian men enthusiastically volunteer as if they were about to set off on the greatest of adventures, the Australians were decidedly less enthused about this latest brewing conflict. It's said that only twenty thousand Australians volunteered in the opening stages of this war, even though Britain was putting pressure on Australia to come up with a formidable fighting force by the fall of 1939.

However, during the interwar period, Australia had lowered its capability to orchestrate a robust military effort. In truth, the Australians had become too dependent on the British Royal Navy. The British, as overstretched as they were, soon became unable to provide a robust protection of Australian interests. By the summer of 1940, France had already been knocked out of the war, and Britain was looking for any help it could find. Initially, the military planners desired to have Australians shipped over to France, just like in World War I, but France's quick capitulation changed those plans. There would be no repeat like the Western Front of World War I in this quick-moving war.

After the fall of France, Italy's dictator, Benito Mussolini, officially threw in his lot with Hitler and declared war on Britain. This meant that Australia was at war with Italy as well. Italy's entry into the war opened up a whole new front since Italy had extensive colonial holdings in North Africa. Many of them, such as Italy's colonial holdings in Libya, butted right up against British colonial territory. British outposts in Egypt and Sudan were now wedged between Italian Libya and Italian-occupied Ethiopia. Threatened on all sides, the British deployed in North Africa desperately needed an influx of reinforcements. The Australians provided this boost to British morale.

Australians and troops from British-controlled India poured into the region in November 1940. The Australians fought hard. In early 1941, they enjoyed a string of victories, such as the Battle of Bardia on January 3rd, the Battle of Tobruk on January 22nd, and the Battle of Benghazi on February 7th. The Australians are said to have suffered some 130 deaths in the Battle of Bardia alone. Nevertheless, this battle was viewed as a stunning success and was a great morale booster since it was able to bring back a sense of forward momentum among the Allied troops, who had been increasingly put on the defensive ever since the fall of France.

The Allies (which at that point consisted mostly of Britain, the freedom fighters of Free France, and dominion troops such as the Australians) were literally on the march. They were battling it out in the Mediterranean Sea. Australian naval forces took on Italian ships and submarines. The Italian submarines tried their best to keep British and Australian craft at bay but were ultimately outdone. Several Italian submarines were sunk.

With more freedom to move across the shorelines of North Africa, Australian naval craft were able to punish Italian positions on the ground with naval bombardments from the water. This proved a great aid to future ground operations against Italian positions.

Along with taking on the Italians, the Australian forces also attempted to open up a second front in Africa by taking on the forces of Vichy France. Vichy France was the rump state that had formed in southern France around the town of Vichy, France, after France's defeat at the hands of the Germans. This French government was essentially a German puppet state. Although it claimed neutrality, it was a passive ally of Germany; as such, the British and Australians viewed Vichy France as a legitimate target.

The battlecruiser *Australia* made its way to French-controlled Senegal and tried to seize this piece of prized wartime territory from Vichy France. The French fighters positioned there showed that they would not be easily overcome. They put up such a stiff resistance that the plan was aborted, and the Australian battlecruiser retreated.

One of the most notable successes of the Australian fleet in the region occurred on July 19th, 1941. On this day, the Australian battleship *Sydney* managed to sink the Italian battleship *Bartolomeo Colleoni*. This battleship was named after the famed captain general of the Republic of Venice, who had the same name. Bartolomeo Colleoni went down in history as one of the most brilliant Italian tacticians. The fact that his namesake ship was sunk and destroyed likely seemed like a bad omen to the Italians.

The Italians seemed to be fighting a losing battle at this point, and around this time, they were being beaten on an entirely different front. The Italians had shot across the Mediterranean and attempted an ill-prepared invasion of Greece. The invasion was first launched in the fall of 1940, but by the spring of 1941, the Greeks were steadily pushing the Italians out. It seemed as if the Italians were in for a humiliating defeat until the Germans poured in to reinforce Italian positions. Like the movement of chess pieces on a wartime chessboard, this change of dynamics in Greece soon affected the North African theater as well.

The British sought to avoid a complete collapse of Greece and felt compelled to send their own troops to fight off the Germans and Italians in Greece. They also made sure to bring some Australian troops with them. The Australian 6th Division was sent to Greece that April.

However, this repositioning of troops meant that positions in North Africa would become more vulnerable. This increasing vacuum meant greater demands were placed on the Australians to fill in the gaps. Even more young Australian men were sent abroad into these increasingly volatile theaters of war.

In some ways, Australian leadership felt as if the Australian armed forces were being yanked around a bit too much by the British high command. They also did not feel as if they were being appreciated for all of the efforts they were making. The growing feelings of frustration led Australian Prime Minister Robert Menzies to head to London in 1941 to discuss how the war was shaping up. During the course of this discussion, Robert Menzies suggested that British Prime Minister Winston Churchill should give the Australians more independence when it came to British decision-making. He even suggested establishing a special war cabinet of dominion leaders such as himself.

Menzies was disappointed in Churchill's reaction. At times, Churchill was rather dismissive. He seemed to think that the Australian armed forces should be at the beck and call of the British and have no say from their own Australian leadership. Australian leadership had traditionally deferred to the British, but there was an increasing desire to position Australian forces closer to home to defend the Australian mainland.

These feelings sharpened to a razor's edge in December of 1941 when Japan went on the offensive and bombed a US naval base in Hawaii. Several Japanese battalions made landfall in Singapore on February 8th, 1942. Just prior to the Japanese invasion, British forces in the region had been supplemented by an additional two thousand Australian troops on January 24th. The Australian troops were not given a very prominent role in this struggle and were often relegated to backup and fallback positions. The British would later lodge many complaints about the Australian recruits, claiming that they behaved in an unprofessional manner and that there were widespread incidents of drunkenness among them.

Whatever was going on, it seemed that the Australian contingent was not happy being in Singapore and not happy with the roles that the British had given them in this struggle against the Japanese. It was almost as if they were reliving the animosity of their penal colony days when Australian convict settlers stood at odds with distinguished British officers. To put it simply, the Australians and the British rubbed each other the wrong way.

British complaints about their Australian auxiliaries became even more cutting in the last hours of Singapore's defense. There were accusations of Australians abandoning their posts and even attempting to requisition naval craft in order to escape the battle. In the end, Singapore was lost to the British. The British lost an important outpost in the region as a result.

The Japanese could now drive deep, right into Australia's own backyard, with very little to hinder their progress. The overstretched British had already cut their losses. They determined that it was in their best interest to focus most of their effort against Adolf Hitler in Europe and North Africa. So, Japan's aggression was essentially placed on the back burner.

Such a thing might have been in the best interest of Britain, which was attempting to stave off an all-out invasion of the British Isles by German forces, but it certainly was not in the best interest of the Australians. They knew that Japan was their most immediate and dire threat to their own national survival.

Britain and Australia, which had once been firmly joined together, began what could be termed a long and complicated divorce. Instead of turning toward the already overloaded British for support, the Australians turned toward the Americans. The Americans proved better capable of fighting a two-front war. As the US Armed Forces launched an invasion of North Africa to assist the British in taking on German and Italian troops, they also quickly reconstituted their navy and sent a formidable fighting force into the Pacific to try to halt the Japanese advance.

Around this time, a Labor Party candidate named John Curtin rose to the office of prime minister. He lifted the curtain on the growing drift from Britain and looked toward the United States in this existential conflict. Prime Minister Curtin declared, "Without any inhibitions of any kind, I make it quite clear that Australia looks to America, free of any pangs as to our traditional links of kinship with the United Kingdom."[i]

Further cementing this shift away from Britain was the fact that Australia declared war on Japan without consulting Britain. Previously, such a thing would have been unheard of, but considering the dire straits that Australia was in, any outside observer could understand why such an action was taken. In light of the Japanese onslaught, Australia was in a fight for its very survival.

This break with London seemed to have been further formalized a short time later with the Statute of Westminster Adoption Act, which was adopted in 1942. The statute had been introduced several years prior and called for a move toward Australian sovereignty. The 1942 statute made such dreams a reality. It was this statute that enabled Australia to have full control over its foreign affairs, including the ability to declare war on foreign nations if necessary (even though in practice Australia had already done so against Japan). With the threat of outside invasion imminent and with Britain seemingly unable to render appropriate aid, Australia made up its mind to handle its own affairs and finally ratified the statute.

The Japanese ramped up their attacks in the region, raiding both Darwin and Sydney. Even worse, they occupied Papua New Guinea, just to Australia's north. As the Americans slowly moved across the Pacific, Australia became an important outpost. It was viewed as a fallback position in the midst of the bloody carnage that was taking place.

US General Douglas MacArthur would take control of military operations in the region in March 1942. By this time, the Japanese had installed themselves in Papua New Guinea, and by September 1942, they were within marching distance of the modern-day capital of Papua New Guinea, Port Moresby. Australian troops, along with local Papuan auxiliaries, engaged in ferocious battles with the Japanese to stop their advance.

One of these fateful battles was the Battle of Kokoda Track, which is said to have killed some twelve thousand Japanese. The Japanese apparently got the worst of it, as only an estimated two thousand Australians perished. This was, of course, a huge loss of life, but the number was nowhere near as staggering as what the Japanese had

---

[i] West, Barbara A. *A Brief History of Australia*. 2010. Pg. 34.

suffered.

The battles were quite ferocious, and much of the fighting was infused with an intense hatred. The Australians had a special animosity for the Japanese, whom they often likened to "wild beasts." The fact the Japanese were notoriously brutal to any prisoners of war they captured did not do much to diminish this ferocious and beastly image. The Japanese were known to defy conventional wartime standards as it pertained to the treatment of prisoners of war, starving, beating, and making them march for long hours until they dropped dead.

An Australian machine gun team in Wewak, Papua New Guinea.[16]

The fighting against the Japanese in Papua New Guinea was the most significant land campaign for the Australian armed forces during this conflict. After Japan was halted by the United States at the bloody Battle of Midway, ending their advance across the Pacific, the Australians were relegated to a largely auxiliary and even a kind of "mop-up" role. They had to defer to the United States in any matters of importance. When the war came to a close in 1945, Australia was not privy to talks of how the postwar world would shape up.

After it was all said and done, the Australians lost around thirty-seven thousand troops. Many Australians had been taken as prisoners of war.

It is said that of the estimated twenty-two thousand Australians to be captured by the Japanese, only a mere fourteen thousand would live to be repatriated back to Australia at the war's conclusion.

These prisoners of war were used as slave labor by the Japanese to build roads, railroad tracks, and other infrastructure. Many of these unfortunate souls were literally worked to death. One can only imagine how cruel of a sight it must have been to see an emaciated Australian prisoner of war being forced at gunpoint to hammer away at a set of railroad tracks, only to suddenly give out and collapse.

Dutch and Australian prisoners of war in Thailand.[17]

Along with the hardships faced by Australian troops, the average Australian also had to endure the hardships of war—albeit in a much milder variation—such as the shortages of supplies, increased prices for food, rent, and services, and the constant fear of invasion.

After the war, Australia took on a greater role on the world stage. With the help of the US and its Lend-Lease Program, they were able to rebuild and, perhaps even more importantly, modernize. The United States ultimately provided more help in this regard than the British had previously supplied and would continue to do so in the decades to come.

Chapter 9: Immigration, Revitalization, and the Shaping of Modern Australia

In the aftermath of World War II, Australians not only had to rebuild the lagging infrastructure of their nation but also had to come to grips with what it actually meant to be Australian. Australians questioned their convict roots, their status as European supplanters, Aboriginal rights, and new waves of immigrants. Who were they? And more importantly, who did they want to be as a nation?

It was around this time that Australian politicians, such as Labor Party leader Arthur Calwell, began speaking of the so-called "New Australians." This was a term used to describe the forces that were shaping modern Australia. Calwell was an advocate for immigration in order to bolster Australia, which he viewed as being significantly underpopulated. However, there was a catch in Calwell's plans for immigration. He advocated—and later implemented as minister for immigration—the White Australia policy.

An anti-immigration cartoon published in 1888.[18]

The White Australia Policy was one of the most defining and controversial policies in Australian history. First introduced in 1901, it was designed to keep Australia "white" by severely restricting non-European immigration. Through harsh laws like the Immigration Restriction Act, the government ensured that Chinese, Pacific Islanders, and other non-White migrants were excluded from the country.

For decades, Australia remained almost exclusively Anglo-European, rejecting even Jewish refugees fleeing Nazi Germany in the 1930s. However, after World War II, pressure began to build. After the war, most immigrants were displaced refugees fleeing war-ravaged regions of Europe. Many of these immigrants from Europe were Jewish survivors of the Holocaust. According to historian Stuart Macintyre's analysis, in the decade following World War II, Australia welcomed about a million immigrants, with a large majority of them coming from Germany, Greece, the Netherlands, and Italy.

Australia also saw an increase in Chinese migration, particularly from refugees fleeing communist China after 1949. However, many faced resistance, as Australia's White Australia Policy was still in effect, restricting non-European immigration.

Australians were clearly trying to reinforce their perceived European heritage with their immigration policy. Nevertheless, Australians were becoming more keenly aware that they were an outpost of European descendants in a largely non-European region. The sudden independence of neighboring Indonesia only seemed to highlight that point.

Prior to World War II, Indonesia was controlled by the Dutch. In fact, it was referred to as the Dutch East Indies. The Japanese made short work of that when they invaded and occupied the Indonesian archipelago. Even after the Japanese were defeated and kicked out, the Dutch were unable to regain control.

The locals were tired of being lorded over by foreigners and were ready to take matters into their own hands. They launched a brief war of independence in 1947 and successfully sent the Dutch packing. Australia now had a neighboring country that was both non-European and non-Christian (Indonesia is a Muslim-majority country).

Religious preferences did not concern Australians during this period. However, Marxist ideologies raised alarm bells. China officially became communist in 1949, and the Cold War between the Marxist ideologies of the communist bloc versus the capitalist and democratic ideals of the Western world (including Australia) was just getting started.

Even though a war had just ended, there were many in Australia and much of the rest of the world who could not help but wonder when the next conflict would begin. The creation of nuclear weapons led to concern that this conflict could be much more devastating. It was for this reason that Australia began to look toward the newly formed United Nations to try to avert a potential calamity of epic proportions.

The Cold War had just erupted, and due to their past experience of being caught by surprise by external aggression, there were many nervous Australian officials who began to look anxiously toward the Soviet Union and China. Although both of these nations were allies during World War II, communist ideology made them potential adversaries in the eyes of capitalist nations.

China was still in the infancy of its communist transformation but was likely more threatening to Australians because of its closer proximity. To this day, China presents a grave threat to Australia. Australia has even partnered with its one-time enemy Japan (along with the United States) as a means to deter communist China.

Nevertheless, immigrants continued to be drawn to Australia, largely because of the stability of its governance and economic opportunities. The new immigrants who arrived on Australian shores found Australia in the midst of a postwar industrial boom. Many people found jobs in manufacturing-based industries or major public works projects. The building of hydroelectric dams and other kinds of power stations used these new immigrants as a source of labor.

Between 1945 and 1985, around four million immigrants relocated to Australia. Many countries around the world actively tried to limit immigration, so Australia's eagerness to increase the number of immigrants was rather unique. Also, by the 1960s, the White Australia Policy was being slowly dismantled. By 1973, the White Australia Policy was officially abolished, and in the years that followed, Australia became one of the most multicultural nations in the world.

Sydney sometime around 1945.[19]

However, these so-called "New Australians" were not always welcomed by the Old Australians. Nevertheless, the labor pool was certainly welcome and arrived at a crucial juncture. Europe was still crawling out of the rubble, wreck, and ruin of the last world war. While their European peers were trying to rebuild, Australia was given a grand opportunity to finally catch up and climb the industrial ladder. Determined to become an industrial hub, Australia was able to build a wide variety of factories to produce all manner of goods that could be exported all over the world.

During the dark and uncertain days of the Cold War, Australia also made the most of its newfound partnership with the United States. In 1951, a formal coalition was created between Australia, New Zealand, and the United States, which was referred to as ANZUS. This was a security pact in which all parties agreed to take action if any one of them were attacked. Many in the Australian public were relieved to have the protection of the United States military in case an external threat ever arose. This pact would remain in force over the next several decades. The United States suspended its obligations to New Zealand in 1986, but as of this writing, it remains in force between Australia and the United States.

With their security seemingly assured, Australians—both of the old and the new variety—entered into a period of prosperity. The Australian economy of the 1950s and 1960s was booming. Fueled by post-war reconstruction, rapid industrialization, and a growing workforce, the nation entered a period of unprecedented prosperity. The economy grew at an average rate of over 4 percent per year, and for much of the 1960s, unemployment sat at a remarkable low of just 1.5 percent to 2.5 percent.

Manufacturing was on the rise, with industries producing everything from automobiles to household appliances. The Holden car, first produced in 1948, became a symbol of Australia's industrial success, and by the 1960s, there was one car for every 3.5 Australians—an astonishing leap from 1 per 14 people in 1946.

Australia's wealth was also tied to its vast natural resources. Exports of wool, wheat, and minerals surged, helping the nation establish strong trade ties with Asia and beyond. By the late 1960s, Australia had transformed into a modern industrial economy, setting the stage for its continued growth in the decades to come.

However, the Cold War conflict in Vietnam forced the Australians to make good on their pact with the United States. As the United States became more involved in the battlefields of Southeast Asia, Australia was expected to contribute to the war effort.

The Australian government first began by sending military advisors. In the late 1960s, Australian troops put their boots on the ground. It is said that by 1967, there were 6,300 Australians fighting in Vietnam. These Australians came from all walks of life and from all backgrounds.

These Australians—just like their American counterparts—soon began to hear all kinds of dreadful news reports of just how bloody and seemingly intractable the Vietnam conflict was. Australian battalions withstood the infamous Tet Offensive in late 1968, which saw both the North Vietnamese troops and their underground auxiliaries, the Viet Cong, join forces to stage a surprise massive assault deep in the heart of South Vietnam. The Australians and their allies stood strong and ultimately beat their opponents back, but it came at a bloody cost. Even worse, much of the carnage on the ground was widely documented and seemed to solidify the notion in the public's mind that Vietnam was an unwinnable war.

After several years of fighting, it seemed that the war was nowhere near the end. No one likes it their nation's youth is killed and maimed in what seems to be an endless and seemingly unwinnable war. Considering as much, protests began to bubble up in Australia. In 1968, the younger generations began to mobilize in the streets to protest Australia's involvement in Vietnam. These protests later crystallized in 1970, as large-scale demonstrations were held in opposition to the war. The younger generation's vocal opposition to the war and a new set of liberal values began to reshape modern Australian society.

The protest against the war led to other social activism, such as Australia's women's liberation movement, which came to prominence in Adelaide in 1969. The 1970s also saw a revitalized movement for Aboriginal rights. Yes, both new and old Australians alike would have a hand in shaping the Australia we know today.

Chapter 10: The Economy and Environmental and Political Challenges

"When my father was alive, this is what he taught me. He had taught me traditional ways like traditional designs in the body or head of kangaroo Dreaming (that's what we call marlu Dreaming) and eagle Dreaming. He taught me how to sing songs for the big ceremonies. People who are related to us in a close family, they have the have the same sort of jukurrpa Dreaming, and to sing songs in the same way as we do our actions like dancing and paintings on our body or shields or things, and this is what my father taught me. My Dreaming is the kangaroo Dreaming, the eagle Dreaming and the budgerigar Dreaming, so I have three kinds of Dreaming in my jukurrpa and I have to hang onto it."

-Paddy Japaljarri

In the latter half of the 20th century, Australia faced plenty of challenges. US President Jimmy Carter was struggling to get a grip on rising gas and grocery store prices in the late 1970s. The Australian economy faced strikingly similar issues of inflation.

During this period, the Australian economy was wide open to outside investors, leading to an increase in privatization. Economic matters, in

---

[1] Macintyre, Stuart. A Concise History of Australia. 1999. Pg. 10.

general, had taken on a much more global scope. Australia even became closer partners with many East Asian countries.

Part of the stability that Australia enjoyed during this period can be attributed to the fact that its two main political parties were not all that different. They had some differences, to be sure, but as it pertained to major policies that would affect the Australian way of life, they both tended to go down a middle road. According to writer and historian John H. Chambers, a strong sense of Australian nationalism prevailed amongst the majority of Australians after Gough Whitlam's Labor government in the mid-1970s.

Gough Whitlam was an interesting figure, to say the least. He was often described as a big man with a lot of big ideas. Whitlam imparted upon Australia a heady dose of new legislation aimed at taking the Australian homeland to the world stage.

Whitlam was seen as an ingenious orator with an incredible wit. He always seemed to know exactly the right thing to say at the right moment, and he absolutely dominated Australian politics. As historian Geoffrey Blainey once put it, "he could not ride a wave without commanding it to halt or accelerate."[i]

In his first few months, Whitlam had several diplomatic achievements, such as opening Australia's doors to China and even Vietnam. This was an interesting feat since Australia had sent troops to fight in Vietnam not long before. Whitlam actually oversaw the final remnants of Australian troops be removed from Vietnam.

Gough Whitlam took note of the protest movement and decided to go even further than that. He heeded the calls of the youth and completely got rid of the military draft. He also made them happy by getting rid of fees to attend college.

Whitlam and his party spent quite a bit of money to create new and attractive social programs. Some of his contemporary critics, as well as critics today, might decry that these programs are nothing more than a bit of political chicanery to conjure up votes by giving free handouts to constituents.

Even though such things might have been incredibly appealing at the time, they were rather short-sighted. The Australian public would learn

---

[i] Blainey, Geoffrey. *A Shorter History of Australia.* 1994. Pg. 221.

that nothing was truly free. Shifting money from one place to another just created a different kind of financial burden. These efforts—no matter how popular they might have been—only helped to add to the ever-increasing level of inflation. It might have been a noble effort to funnel money into social welfare programs to help the poor, but if these same programs make the price of bread go through the roof by way of inflation, they really are not helping anyone in the long run.

Nevertheless, there were many who felt that such programs were needed, not only for the uplifting of citizens but also for the conservation of the environment. During this period, great conservation efforts were made. Large sections of the Outback were converted into national parks.

There was also a growing awareness of just how fragile Australia's environment could be. In 1983, a terrible spate of wildfires erupted. These fires led to the deaths of around seventy-five people and were extremely taxing on Australian rescue services. Wildfires continue to be a major problem for Australians to this day.

Vital national resources were being discovered in the meantime. For example, huge diamond deposits were found in the vicinity of Kimberly in Western Australia. There were also discoveries of oil and natural gas, which were soon being pumped into huge pipelines all the way to Perth.

Sizeable grants were put together for the sake of preserving old buildings deemed to have some sort of historical significance. Along with setting aside land for national parks and preserving historic buildings, the Australian government also established large tracts of land for the Aboriginals by allocating large portions of the Northern Territory to them.

There was a resurgence of Australian nationalism during this time. In many ways, it would perhaps be better to describe it as the discovery of Australian nationalism. Australia was so linked to Britain for much of its history that any sense of patriotism was a British sense of patriotism. But now Australians were suddenly trying to find themselves. The Australians discarded old distinctions in favor of new, entirely Australian ones. The Order of Australia was created to award extraordinary Australian citizens with an entirely Australian honor. This prestigious award is available to any Australian citizen who has proven themselves by performing some form of outstanding service or achievement.

These nationalistic overtures continued to take hold even in the midst of (and perhaps in spite of) an immigration boom that took off in the

1980s. Many immigrants came from Vietnam. Ever since the end of the war in Vietnam, several waves of people, who were often derisively dubbed the "boat people," showed up on Australian shores. It is estimated that by the year 1985, eighty thousand Vietnamese had come to Australia. By 2011, that number had increased to 180,000.

Vietnam was not the only part of the world that saw a massive influx of refugees head to Australia. The Lebanese Civil War, which lasted from 1975 to 1990, prompted quite a few refugees to seek a safer place to live. Most of these refugees were Greek Orthodox and Maronite Catholic, although some were also of the Muslim faith. No matter their religious background, all were seeking an escape from violence.

Chinese dissidents also sought asylum in Australia in the late 1980s. Many Chinese students were already in Australia on student visas when the Tiananmen Square protest occurred in China in 1989. During this infamous protest/revolt, a large group of mostly college-aged students tried to stand up to the communist government of China. Many communist regimes were falling apart in Eastern Europe during this time, and it seemed that these Chinese protesters were seeking a similar scenario in China. But that is not what happened.

The Chinese government cracked down with fury, and the protesters were met with machine guns and tanks. In consideration of the safety of the Chinese dissidents already in Australia on student visas, the Australian government agreed to allow many of these student visas to be converted into residential visas so that these students could effectively stay in Australia and remain safe from China's wrath.

Interestingly enough, in that same fateful year of 1989, Australia first went online. Australia was linked to the internet for the first time by way of the Australian Academic Research Network, which connected the University of Melbourne across the Pacific all the way to the University of Hawaii. Back in those days, the internet was largely used by universities for research purposes. This particular linkup was just the first step in Australia's internet usage.

Australia was rapidly changing, but even so, in 1988, a special bicentennial was held to celebrate two hundred years since the first Anglo settlers had arrived. This was celebrated on January 26th, 1988, to mark the two-hundredth anniversary of Captain Arthur Phillip's landing and the founding of the Australian colony of New South Wales. The Aboriginals of Australia decided that this date would be more aptly described as a day of mourning rather than anything to celebrate since it marked the end of their cultural dominance of the continent.

In many ways, Australians are still in the process of finding themselves. In a land of such diverse backgrounds and points of view, it is indeed hard to define exactly what it means to be Australian. In the 1980s, the *Mad Max* and *Crocodile Dundee* films tried to identify Australia with the rugged Outback and rugged masculinity.

Australia, unfortunately, was lambasted with more than its fair share of unintentional stereotypes. In August 1980, an Australian woman by the name of Lindy Chamberlain claimed that a dingo took her baby from her while she had been camping with her baby. She reportedly exclaimed, "A dingo's got my baby!"

The press ate it up, and Lindy was steadfastly disbelieved and roundly ridiculed. Some thought perhaps she had done something to the child and made up a goofy story about a dingo to cover it up. She was ultimately charged with the baby girl's murder and spent time in prison before the authorities realized that she was telling the truth. In 1986, the police discovered the child's bloody clothing in a dingo's nesting grounds. It was truly tragic what Lindy had to go through, both losing a child and being falsely accused of her child's demise. She and Australians as a whole also had to endure the stereotypical laughter of non-Australians asking them in a fake Australian accent, "So, did the dingo get your baby?"

The joke was still being used in the early 1990s; even the show *Seinfeld* used the line as a joke. Elaine mocked an Australian character in one episode. Apparently annoyed by the Australian, Elaine threw her off balance by suddenly proclaiming, "Maybe the Dingo ate your baby!"

This moment became iconic, but it was still a sad bit of stereotyping all the same. And the search for what it really meant to be an Australian—all mockery aside—would continue in full force. This search for national discovery was done by both European transplants and the descendants of Aboriginal people groups.

In the 1990s, Labor Prime Minister Paul Keating took a historic step in recognizing Aboriginal land rights with the passage of the Native Title Act. This landmark law, passed in December 1993, set up tribunals to determine which lands in Australia could be rightfully claimed by Aboriginal and Torres Strait Islander peoples.

The results were significant. Large portions of Australia's landmass were found to have potential Native title claims, sparking heated debates between Indigenous groups, farmers, and mining companies. However, while some early estimates suggested that over half of the continent could be subject to claims, many areas, such as private property and developed land, were excluded.

By 1998, more than seven hundred claims had been filed as Indigenous groups sought to reclaim their heritage and connection to their country. However, the process was slow, complex, and often frustrating. Many claims took years to resolve, requiring extensive historical, cultural, and legal proof to be recognized.

Much of the land under the Native claim was remote, rugged, and difficult to develop, but for Indigenous Australians, these places remained deeply significant. Even today, vast stretches of the Australian Outback remain uninhabited, not because of Native title claims but because of the harsh conditions and isolation.

There was a significant backlash among more conservative-leaning Australians in the meantime. They felt that the Australian government was going too far in appeasing Aboriginal rights groups. They found their voice in a populist political figure named Pauline Hanson. She was first elected to Parliament as an independent in 1996. She pushed back against some of the growing trends of multiculturalism and calls for Aboriginal rights. She decried what she described as government handouts to Aboriginals and claimed that Australians of European descent were being discriminated against in favor of benefiting minority groups such as the Aboriginals.

Pauline Hanson is a complicated figure, with some denouncing her as a narrow-minded bigot and others believing that she was a realist who was not afraid to speak her mind. In her opening speech in Parliament, she described herself as the ultimate outsider. She stated that she was just an everyday Australian woman seeking to make her nation better. Her critics, of course, never bought into this.

The modern era of Australia could be said to have truly begun under the leadership of Australian Prime Minister John Howard. He was elected prime minister in 1996 and served until 2007. He presided over a powerful Liberal-National Party coalition. This coalition instituted massive legislation for gun control and industry. They also overhauled taxation.

John Howard.[30]

Not all of these measures were popular with everyone. At the start of John Howard's time as prime minister, tensions erupted into one of the most chaotic protests in Australian political history. On August 19th, 1996, thousands of union workers and Indigenous activists gathered outside Parliament House in Canberra, rallying against Howard's industrial relations policies and cuts to Indigenous programs.

What began as a peaceful demonstration soon spiraled out of control. A group of protesters stormed the front entrance, forcing their way into the Parliament House foyer and clashing with police. In the chaos, sixty police officers were injured, and fifty protesters were arrested.

A year after this dramatic unrest, populist parliamentarian Pauline Hanson managed to establish a political party of her own making, the One Nation Party. The group was popular and soon had members in excess of twenty-five thousand. In the 1998 election, the One Nation Party won nearly a quarter of the vote.

John Howard and his party were beset with questions about Australia's future identity as a governing entity. One of the more frequent questions was about when Australia would completely cut its links with Britain. Even though Australia was ostensibly independent and fully capable of handling its own affairs, the British monarch was still technically considered the head of state. As of this writing, Britain still has a say over the governor-general, who is appointed to represent the British monarch.

Howard created some trouble in 2001 when he appointed an Anglican archbishop to the role of governor-general. This selection was problematic for a variety of reasons. For one, many disagreed with having a bishop in the role due to the Australian notion of separation of church and state. More trouble erupted when it was revealed that the bishop had overseen investigations into previous sex abuse incidents in the church and had not handled it well. Hollingworth ultimately resigned in May 2003, becoming the first governor-general in Australian history to step down due to scandal.

Big changes were on the way later that year. Terrorists decided to strike multiple targets in the United States. The World Trade Center was destroyed in New York, and the Pentagon was badly damaged when terrorists hijacked planes and flew them into the targets. A third target was averted when passengers took matters into their own hands and attempted to storm the cockpit. The terrorists ended up taking the plane down in an empty field in Pennsylvania as a result. The passengers were killed, but they went down as heroes since they had thwarted the terrorists. It is widely believed that the terrorists who had hijacked this plane intended to send it crashing into either the US Capitol building or perhaps even the White House itself.

That fateful day in September day led to the War on Terror. Under George W. Bush, the American government was ready to exact vengeance, and their strategic partner Australia did not hesitate to lend a hand. The United States, after all, had suffered what seemed to be an entirely unprovoked attack (although some die-hard ideologues might try to argue that point), and most Australians were rather enthusiastic to show their support.

Australians would be involved in the subsequent US-led invasion of Afghanistan, which occurred as a result of the 9-11 attack. Afghanistan was not chosen at random. The Taliban regime of Afghanistan had sheltered and shielded the terrorist group al-Qaeda, which had orchestrated the attacks on the US. Immediately after the attack, the Bush administration demanded that the Taliban turn over the al-Qaeda terrorists who were responsible, and they refused. This was considered more than enough reason to launch a war against the Taliban regime.

Australian forces operating in Uruzgan during the War on Terror.[21]

The goal was to root out the terrorists, punish the Taliban, and attempt a regime change. After the disastrous pullout of US troops under President Joe Biden in 2021, some twenty years after the Taliban had initially been dismantled, all of these efforts came to naught since a resurgent Taliban resumed control of this troubled region.

At any rate, as it pertains to Australia's efforts in 2001, Australian armed forces were on the ground in Afghanistan, along with British and American troops. Shortly thereafter, US President Bush decided to up the ante by declaring that other countries could face preemptive strikes if it was believed they were harboring terrorist cells. Essentially, he was alluding to a potential strike against Iraq.

Australian Prime Minster Howard also began to speak in a very similar manner. He suggested that Australia should intervene in another country's affairs if they were found to be somehow harboring terrorists. This stance would be significantly challenged on October 12th, 2002, when a terrorist group bombed a nightclub in Bali in nearby Indonesia. This attack left eighty-eight Australians dead. Would Australia go to war with Indonesia?

Such a thing would be unthinkable. An Australian-Indonesian war would be devastating for both parties, as well as the surrounding region. Fortunately, it did not come to that since the Indonesian government was entirely forthcoming and cooperative in helping to hunt down the terrorists. As such, regime change was never on the menu in this instance.

This was not the case in Sadam Hussein's case, though. That is not to say that Sadaam was actually harboring terrorists or (as he was also accused) weapons of mass destruction in Iraq. However, Saddam was notoriously combative and non-cooperative with international inspectors. His combative nature seemed to lend credence to many of the Bush administration's accusations. Despite the United Nations attempting to dissuade Bush, the United States launched an invasion of Iraq in 2003.

The Australians, perhaps against their better judgment, stood next to their American allies and took part in this military operation as well. Australian soldiers were there along with American and British troops in March 2003 when the regime of Saddam Hussein was toppled. These allies later found that Saddam did not have weapons of mass destruction, and any supposed links to terrorism remained as dubious as ever. However, Australia did not get the same kind of blame as America and Britain did. America and Britain were seen as the leading antagonists, while Australia appeared to simply be backing them up. Howard had voiced doubt early on and was never wholeheartedly sold on the weapons of mass destruction.

Nevertheless, Australia remained on good terms with the United States. Things were so good that the two nations signed the Australia-United States Free Trade Agreement in 2004.

Interestingly, Howard weighed in on a presidential election in the United States. In 2007, he made some rather pointed remarks about

Barack Obama's candidacy. Obama, who made the Iraq War a big part of his campaign, had spoken of his desire to withdraw US troops from Iraq if he was elected. As soon as Howard heard about this campaign pledge, he cried foul. He declared that such a move would be nothing short of surrender and that al-Qaeda was no doubt rooting for Obama to win the election due to his defeatist sentiment.

Obama did not take the criticism lightly. Around 140,000 US troops were in the region at the time, while Australia only had 1,400 soldiers. Obama suggested that if the Australian prime minister was so eager to continue the war, then he should go ahead and send another twenty thousand Australian soldiers into the war. Prime Minister Howard was unable to meet this challenge.

The long-running Howard government ultimately came to an end in 2007. It was succeeded by Prime Minister Kevin Rudd's government. Rudd helped steer Australia through an economic crisis in 2008. Because of his stewardship, Australia survived the storm. According to data on the subject, Australia fared better than many other countries.

Rudd also addressed the long-standing issue of Aboriginal rights, making it a point to actually go on the record and apologize for past government abuses toward Aboriginal peoples. He especially sought to address the matter of stolen generations, seeking to find forgiveness for the injustices of the past.

Prime Minister Rudd was in charge until 2013, when he was replaced by Tony Abbott. Abbott was replaced by political firebrand Malcolm Turnbull in 2015. Turnbull's government placed a heavy emphasis on relations with China. Turnbull was mainly concerned with Chinese aggression and competitiveness in the South China Sea. Turnbull also turned a wary eye toward Chinese 5G networks being installed in Australia. These Chinese 5G companies were ultimately banned.

Turnbull was out by 2018, and Scott Morrison took charge of Australia's government. Under the Morrison administration, Australia entered into the AUKUS agreement in the fall of 2021. AUKUS is short for "Australia, the United Kingdom, and the United States." This agreement was spearheaded by US President Joe Biden and sought to shore up strategic ties between the United States, the United Kingdom, and Australia to defend the whole Indo-Pacific region.

The initiation of the partnership immediately ignited controversy. Predictably enough, China did not appreciate the move, declaring that the efforts were essentially warmongering and harboring a "Cold War" mentality. But perhaps a bit less predictably, the initiative was also condemned by a Western ally—France.

The French were upset because the US pledged to build nuclear submarines for Australia as part of the deal. The French government felt as if it were thrown under the bus here since it had already contracted with the Australians to build submarines. This sudden change of plans meant the Australians canceled a deal with the French that was reportedly worth as much as ninety billion US dollars.

The French were not only upset that they had lost all of this potential revenue; they were also upset that they were given very little, if any, warning that such a deal was even in the works. This lack of cooperation between the signatories of AUKUS and France was condemned by the French foreign minister, Jean-Yves Le Drian, as nothing short of a stab in the back.

The French were not placated until Prime Minister Morrison was replaced by Anthony Albanese in Australia's 2022 election. Albanese finally settled the matter by agreeing to pay French contractor Naval Group hundreds of millions of dollars in compensation for the scrapped deal with France.

China continues to cast a wary eye on AUKUS and the Indo-Pacific partnership. For China, it is a clear challenge. In particular, it is believed that Australia's acquisition of nuclear-powered submarines would be used as a deterrent in the advent of a Chinese attempt to invade Tawain. Australia is a few thousand miles south of Tawain. That may seem like a good bit of distance, but Australia is certainly much closer than the other two members of AUKUS. Australia and its new nuclear subs one day may be placed on the front lines of a war with China.

China may be frustrated with such a prospect, but segments of Australia are worried about it as well. One dissenting voice, former Deputy Secretary of Defense Hugh White, made remarks in 2024, describing the deal as being fraught with danger for Australia.

White seems to be concerned that Australia will fall into the same old subservient trap that it faced with the British. Certain segments of Australia do not want the nation to be entirely submissive to the interests of a greater power and forced to fight its battles, especially if the conflict goes against Australia's own national interests.

Did the Australians really shake out of the grasp of Britain just to do the bidding of the United States? The implications are indeed huge. And in consideration of much, it remains to be seen what the future holds for Australia, AUKUS, the whole region, and the entire planet.

The phrase "World War Three" has been bandied about in recent years, especially in regard to hotspots such as Eastern Europe and the Middle East. However, the Indo-Pacific region is another flashpoint that could quickly flare up into an all-out global war. As of early 2025, there is still some semblance of peace in the waters surrounding Australia in the Indo-Pacific, but as political and international challenges continue to mount, there is no guarantee that this will remain the case indefinitely.

Conclusion: Australia's Future Foreign Policy

Australia has overcome more than its fair share of challenges. From the beginning, Australian settlers learned to get by in what was a harsh and often hostile environment. They built a robust nation that could stand tall among its global competitors. Australia served with distinction in two world wars and has since played a pivotal part in global affairs.

Most recently, Australia faced a foe that was both formidable and unexpected. Australia was deeply affected by the 2020 pandemic, just like much of the rest of the world. However, Australia showed firm resolve and managed to mitigate the dreaded virus. While much of the rest of the world was reeling from the effects of the coronavirus, Australia was able to undertake measures that greatly reduced the incidence of the disease. Both Australia and nearby New Zealand led the world in recovering from this terrible pandemic.

As much as Australia has been made to follow in the steps of other world powers, such as Britain and the United States, there is an increasing desire for Australia to be able to lead in its own right. The recent AUKUS partnership has seemingly doused gasoline on this passion, resulting in further cries for Australia to take greater hold of its own destiny.

However, for all of this wishful thinking, there are still plenty of pragmatic realists in Australia who realize that the Indo-Pacific region, in which Australia resides, may not always be the friendliest neighborhood.

Australia learned this lesson well enough during World War II when the Japanese landed right in Papua New Guinea.

If the Japanese had won the war, there is little doubt that Australia's future under Japanese hegemony would have been rather grim. Now, there are similar fears about the rising power of China. If there is a war over Tawain, would Australia be left in the middle of it? Or worse, would Australia and its nuclear submarines, courtesy of AUKUS, be forced to fight a war for the United States in an apocalyptic clash of superpowers?

As it pertains to the nation's march into the future, Australia will soon face an incredibly daunting foreign policy fork in the road. Should Australia exert more independent strategic actions? Or should it continue to toe the line in the name of collective security?

There are no easy answers to these questions, and arguments could be raised to support either side of the debate. Australia has always been in a unique position and has long played a unique role in world affairs. This important outpost will undoubtedly continue to be of great importance in the near future.

Here's another book by Enthralling History that you might like

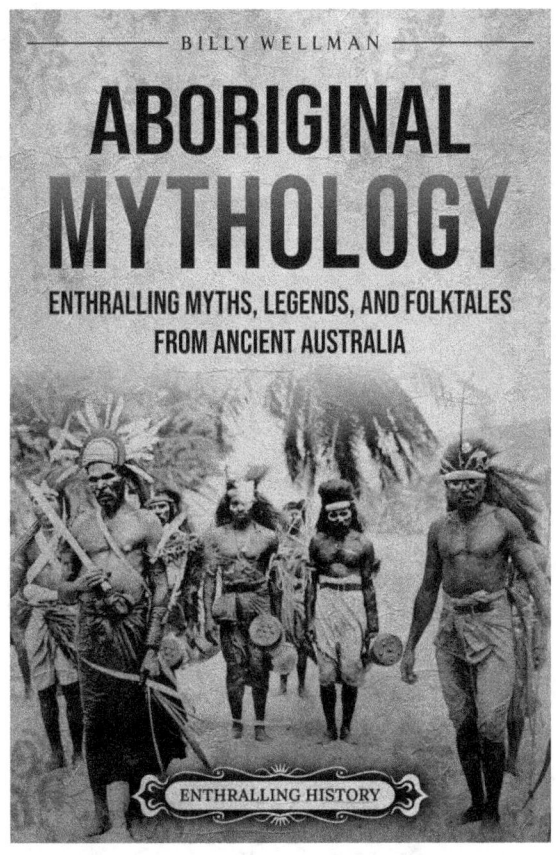

Free limited time bonus

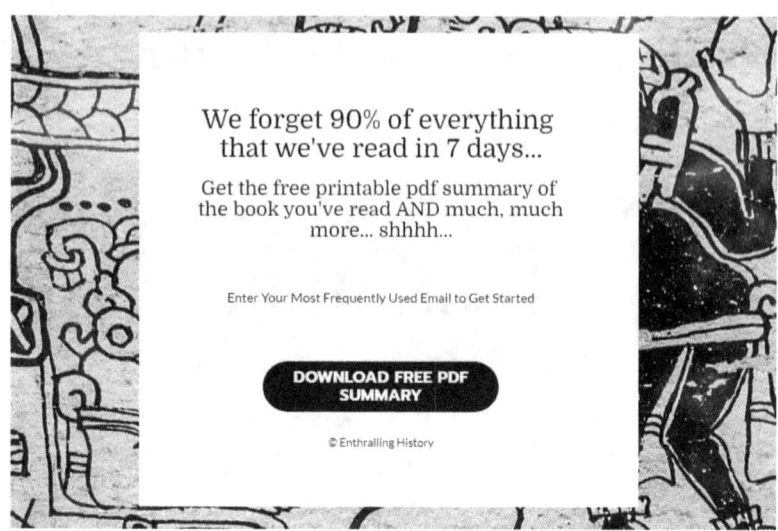

Stop for a moment. We have a free bonus set up for you. The problem is this: we forget 90% of everything that we read after 7 days. Crazy fact, right? Here's the solution: we've created a printable, 1-page pdf summary for this book that you're reading now. All you have to do to get your free pdf summary is to go to the following website: **https://livetolearn.lpages.co/enthrallinghistory/**

Or, Scan the QR code!

Once you do, it will be intuitive. Enjoy, and thank you!

Further Reading and Reference

Blainey, Geoffrey. *A Shorter History of Australia*. 1994.
Chambers, John H. *A Traveler's History of Australia*. 1999.
Clark, Manning. *A History of Australia*. 1988.
Docherty, J. C. *The A to Z of Australia*. 2010.
Grey, Jeffrey. *A Military History of Australia*. 1990.
Macintyre, Stuart. *A Concise History of Australia*. 1999.
Pahoff, Michael. *Australia: A New More Inclusive History*. 2021.
West, Barbara A. *A Brief History of Australia*. 2010.

Image Sources

1 Thomas Schoch (= user Mosmas), CC BY-SA 3.0 <https://creativecommons.org/licenses/by-sa/3.0>, via Wikimedia Commons, https://commons.wikimedia.org/wiki/File:Aboriginal_Art_Australia.jpg
2 https://commons.wikimedia.org/wiki/File:Abel_Tasman_-_Cuyp_(cropped)_(adjusted).jpg
3 Lencer, CC BY-SA 3.0 <https://creativecommons.org/licenses/by-sa/3.0>, via Wikimedia Commons, https://commons.wikimedia.org/wiki/File:Australia_discoveries_by_Europeans_before_1813_en.png
4 https://commons.wikimedia.org/wiki/File:Captainjamescookportrait.jpg
5 https://commons.wikimedia.org/wiki/File:Arthur_Phillip_-_Wheatley_ML124.jpg
6 https://commons.wikimedia.org/wiki/File:Two_of_the_Natives_of_New_Holland,_Advancing_to_Combat.jpg
7 https://commons.wikimedia.org/wiki/File:Alexander_Schramm_-_A_scene_in_South_Australia_-_Google_Art_Project.jpg
8 https://commons.wikimedia.org/wiki/File:WilliamBligh.jpeg
9 https://commons.wikimedia.org/wiki/File:Mr_E.H._Hargraves,_The_Gold_Discoverer_of_Australia,_Feb_12th_1851_returning_the_salute_of_the_gold_miners_-_Thomas_Tyrwhitt_Balcombe.jpg
10 https://commons.wikimedia.org/wiki/File:Landing_at_melbourne_1840.jpg
11 https://commons.wikimedia.org/wiki/File:William_Strutt_Bushrangers.jpg
12 https://commons.wikimedia.org/wiki/File:Ned_Kelly_in_1880.png
13 https://commons.wikimedia.org/wiki/File:HenryParkes_Melbourne.jpg

14 https://commons.wikimedia.org/wiki/File:Australian_9th_and_10th_battalions_Egypt_December_1914_AWM_C02588.jpeg
15 https://commons.wikimedia.org/wiki/File:Menzies_Churchill_WW21941.jpg
16 https://commons.wikimedia.org/wiki/File:Aust_soldiers_Wewak_June_1945.jpg
17 https://commons.wikimedia.org/wiki/File:POWs_Burma_Thai_RR.jpg
18 https://commons.wikimedia.org/wiki/File:Melbourne-Punch-federation-Victoria-pest-Australian-Chinese-May-1888.jpg
19 State Library of New South Wales, No restrictions, via Wikimedia Commons, https://commons.wikimedia.org/wiki/File:Railway_Square,_ca._1945.jpg
20 https://commons.wikimedia.org/wiki/File;John_Howard_May_2006.jpg
21 ISAF Headquarters Public Affairs Office from Kabul, Afghanistan, CC BY 2.0 <https://creativecommons.org/licenses/by/2.0>, via Wikimedia Commons, https://commons.wikimedia.org/wiki/File:Australian_SOTG_wait_for_extraction_2011.jpg

www.ingramcontent.com/pod-product-compliance
Lightning Source LLC
Chambersburg PA
CBHW070339010526
44107CB00004B/559